SITE OF THE
BATTLE
OF
CORYDON
July 9 - 1863

ERECTED BY THE INDIANA CIVIL WAR CENTENNIAL COMMISSION 1963

Library of Congress Cataloging in Publication Data
Conway, W. Fred, Sr.

Corydon - The Forgotten Battle of the Civil War
Library of Congress Catalog Number: 90-084796
ISBN 0-925165-03-4

FBH Publishers, P.O. Box 711, New Albany, IN 47151
© W. Fred Conway, Sr. 1991

Printed in the United States of America.

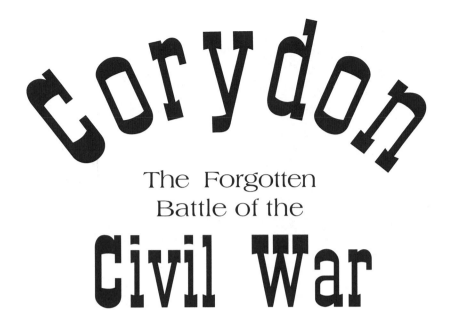

Corydon

The Forgotten
Battle of the

Civil War

W. Fred Conway

The Battle of Corydon, registered by the War Department of the United States Government as an official battle of the Civil War, was one of only two such battles fought on northern soil.* The other battle was the most celebrated one of the war - the Battle of Gettysburg. However, the Corydon battle has been all but forgotten, save by those who live in the area. Hopefully this book will help the "almost forgotten" Civil War battle, fought on northern soil, to regain its rightful place in Civil War history. Within these pages the Battle of Corydon is relived.

* There were various skirmishes in Indiana, Ohio and Pennsylvania, but only Gettysburg and Corydon were termed "Official Battles" by the War Department.

CONTENTS

MAPS

CORYDON
"The Cradle of Indiana"

FIRST • STATE • CAPITOL • BUILDING

Corydon
★

OHIO RIVER

First State Capitol Illustration by Violet Windell. Map/Typography by Andy Markley

Introduction

Corydon, a quaint pioneer village in southern Indiana, was given its name by William Henry Harrison, the ninth President of the United States, who purchased the land for the village in 1804. In Harrison's favorite song, "The Pastoral Elegy", Corydon was the name of the young swain who was "called to dwell in bright mansions on high", leaving his sweetheart to mourn his untimely death. Though Corydon of the song has been long forgotten, the village of Corydon, which was destined soon after its founding to become Indiana's first state capital, has had more than its share of fame over the years.

The same year Harrison bought the land for the new village, Daniel Boone's brother, Squire, built the first grist mill in the area. Daniel and Squire had discovered a beautiful cave near Corydon, and Squire used the torrent of water pouring from its mouth to power the water wheel on his mill. After nearly two centuries, Boone's Mill is still grinding grain, and there are eleven Boone families listed in the Corydon telephone directory.

Around 1811, the uncle of the man destined for greatness as the sixteenth President of the United States moved into the area. Settling a few miles from Corydon was Josiah Lincoln, brother of Thomas Lincoln, who was Abraham Lincoln's father. Abraham Lincoln himself grew up in southern Indiana, only about 40 miles west of Corydon. After nearly two centuries, there are Lincolns still living in the

Corydon area. The telephone directory lists ten families.

In 1813, just five years after the village was platted in 1808, Corydon was chosen to become the territorial capital of Indiana. The new state, formed in 1816, was governed from Corydon until the capital moved to Indianapolis in 1824. During the twelve years Corydon served as Indiana's capital, it was the political, intellectual, and social hub of the state.

But perhaps the most notable event in Corydon's long and colorful history occurred on July 9th, 1863, when the serenity of the peaceful village was shattered by musket and cannon fire. With little warning, the Civil War arrived in Corydon!

Chapter One

Ready For
The Fourth Of July

As summer blossomed in June of 1863 at Corydon, Indiana, the Civil War seemed far away. Five hundred miles to the south, the Battle of Vicksburg was in progress, which seemed remote from Indiana. Five hundred miles to the east, the massive buildup of both northern and southern troops in the area surrounding Gettysburg, Pennsylvania, seemed equally remote.

Though the War Between The States had by now been in progress some two and one half years, the outcome was still uncertain. Both sides had enjoyed major victories and had suffered defeats. At this time, the war easily could have gone either way. President Lincoln would, within the next two weeks, issue a call for a hundred thousand more men to be conscripted from Pennsylvania, Maryland, West Virginia, and Ohio. Indiana was still too far away.

In Corydon, orators were polishing their speeches for the upcoming Fourth of July festivities, while the younger set prepared for the annual Sabbath School basket picnic and dance upon the green. *The Corydon Weekly Democrat* reported that Ben Douglass had been "violently seized and put aboard a steamboat." The fact was that Ben had been seized by his bride and put aboard the steamboat for their honeymoon trip. The newspaper went on to clarify the story: "We congratulate Ben upon his 'arrest and imprisonment'. We hope it will be for life."

The lead article on the front page of the weekly newspaper was devoted to reporting President Lincoln's consultation with a spiritual medium for advice on the war. Quoting from a story in the *Boston Gazette*, the Corydon paper reported that as President Lincoln sat in the darkened Crimson Room of the White House, the medium called up the departed spirits of an Indian, General Henry Knox, George Washington, Lafayette, Benjamin Franklin, Napolean, and various other military leaders. They all seemed to give Lincoln conflicting advice. Lincoln, finally growing disgusted, remarked, "I have seen strange things and heard rather odd remarks, but nothing convinced me that there is anything very heavenly about all this."

The Corydon High School, still in session in June, advertised for students. Monthly tuition for reading and spelling was $1.13, geography or arithmetic $1.35, while algebra, philosophy, or Latin commanded a hefty $2.25.

For anyone who took the trouble to read it, a single paragraph buried at the bottom of the second page of the four page tabloid was a portent of the war encroaching onto northern soil. It read, "The guerrillas last Saturday made a raid into Elizabethtown, Kentucky, and after dispersing the Circuit Court, which was in session, capturing Judge Stewart and stealing what they could get their hands on, left in haste". Elizabethtown, on the other side of the nearby Ohio River, was only about 40 miles away.

Meanwhile, less than 150 miles south of Corydon, at Sparta, Tennessee, Confederate Brigadier General John Hunt Morgan was assembling a rag-tag army totalling 2,460 men. His fame had spread throughout the South, and hun-

GENERAL JOHN HUNT MORGAN

*Known vicariously as "The Thunderbolt of the Confederacy"
and "The Great Horse Thief", the swashbuckling Morgan was
the toast of the Confederacy. His foray into Indiana with some
2,000 "raiders" during July 1863 provided one of the most
colorful dramas of the Civil War.*

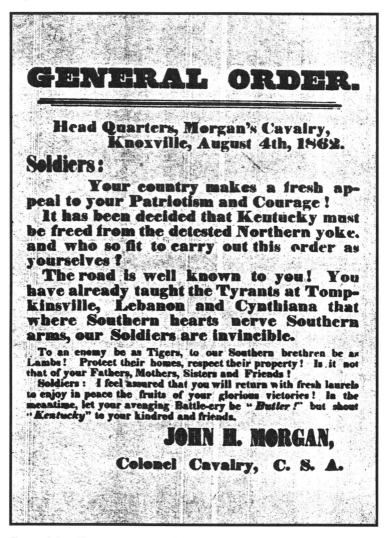

Recruiting Posters prepared by Morgan in 1862 before he had been personally promoted to Brigadier General by Confederate President Jefferson Davis. Morgan's recruiting campaign was overwhelmingly successful, as hundreds of recruits sought the privilege of serving under his command.

PROCLAMATION.

To the Inhabitants of Kentucky!

Fellow Countrymen--

I HAVE KEPT MY PROMISE.

At the head of my old companions in arms, I am once more amongst you, with God's blessing no more to leave you.

Deprived as you are by these Northern Despots of all true information respecting the War, you are probably unaware that our holy Southern cause is everywhere in the ascendant.

The so-called "Young Napoleon," McClellan, has retreated from the Peninsula. Stonewall Jackson, the 'invincible,' is asserting the superiority of our Southern Banner against the armies of Pope, Banks, Fremont, Burnside, and that of McClellan, who has joined them. His ultimate success is assured.

NO POWER ON EARTH CAN MAKE US SLAVES!

Bragg, in Tennessee, is steadily advancing with an overwhelming force on Buel, who is retreating, whilst New Orleans is on the eve of being torn from the clutches of "Butler, the infamous," and restored to its legitimate and Confederate Government.

Kirby Smith at the head of a powerful army, is already in your State, whilst Forrest, Woodward, and myself have already proven to the Yankees our existance by taking Murfreesboro, Gallatin and Clarksville, burning the railroad bridges and damaging seriously the enemy.

AROUSE, KENTUCKIANS! shake off that listless feeling which was engendered by the presence of a powerful and relentless enemy. He is no longer to be feared! We have drawn his eye-teeth! there will soon be nothing left of him but his roar!

Let the old men of Kentucky, and our noble-hearted women, arm their sons and their lovers for the fight! Better death in our sacred cause than a life of slavery!

Young men of Kentucky flock to my standard, it will always wave in the path of honor, and history will relate how you responded to my appeal, and how, by so doing, you saved your country!

JOHN H. MORGAN,

Aug. 22 1862 Col.-Commanding Brigade, C. S. A.

(MORGAN'S PRESS PRINT.)

13

dreds begged to be allowed to serve with him. Some of his men were issued new horses and rifles, but many of them were still riding their own horses and carrying their own muskets, squirrel guns, or pistols. Replacement horses and better weapons eventually would be acquired through the spoils of battle and would be relieved from the northern soldiers they would wound, kill, or capture.

Morgan was no ordinary general. His many nicknames are clues to his magnetic, flamboyant, devil-may-care personality: "The Great Raider", "Our Marion", "The Thunderbolt of the Confederacy", "A True *Beau Sabreur*", "The Great Freebooter", "The Guerrilla Chieftan". He was called by the northerners, "The King of Horse Thieves".

Prior to the war, he had been a businessman in Lexington, Kentucky, and one of his more successful business ventures was slave trading, an activity loathed by Abraham Lincoln. As a young man, Lincoln had been shocked, while on a trip to New Orleans from his home in southern Indiana, to witness slave trading in progress, and he vowed to come down hard against it, if he ever had the chance.

Morgan had been promoted from Colonel to Brigadier General, in person, by Confederate President Jefferson Davis, during the first year of the war. By June of 1863, he had already become one of the south's great heroes. Wearing a plume on his hat, he delighted in such exploits as burning bridges, wrecking railroads, burning commercial establishments, if ransom was not paid, stealing horses, and cleverly deceiving the enemy by starting false rumors, even to the extent of tapping telegraph lines to report where he was heading, only to go off in a different direction. His ruses worked. One of his men described him as follows:

"General Morgan was a magnetic man, of pleasing personality, very handsome, his manner genial and gracious, his face an open book. A dark

14

Jefferson Davis, President of the Confederate States of America, personally promoted Morgan from Colonel to Brigadier General.

moustache drooped over his laughing mouth. His face was lighted by a pleasant, perennial smile. I never saw him other than neatly dressed. His extreme sociability won the hearts of his men and their undying affections. Riding along the column, he would talk in a jovial free and easy way, putting his cavaliers in the best of spirits. He was the 'Marion of the Civil War'."

Not only did Morgan charm his men, the ladies of all ages were smitten by his charms and swooned in his presence. Any southern belle would have considered her fondest dream fulfilled if she could have become his bride. One of them did have her dream come true. Just six months prior

15

Pretty 21-year-old "Mattie" Ready became the bride of 37-year-old John Hunt Morgan on December 14, 1862. The marriage took place in the Ready home in Murfreesboro, Tennessee, which was decorated with "holly and winterberries". The wedding feast included turkeys, hams, chickens, ducks, and "all the delicacies and good dishes of a southern kitchen." Two regimental bands provided music.

to assembling his troops at Sparta, 37-year-old General Morgan married 21-year-old Martha ("Mattie") Ready of Murfreesboro, Tennessee.* As far as is recorded, Morgan remained completely true to his beloved Mattie as long as he lived.

Morgan's immediate superior was General Braxton Bragg, and the two not only disagreed on tactics; they disagreed on virtually everything. Bragg so disliked the brash Morgan that his feeling toward him was almost one of hatred. Not only did Bragg twice refuse permission for Morgan to visit Mattie, who was now pregnant; he even recommended to Confederate President Jefferson Davis that no further promotions be given to Morgan because he was "a dangerous man on account of his intense desire to act independently." Conversely, Morgan had so little respect for Bragg that he conceived a daring plan, which totally disregarded Bragg's firm order: "Do not cross the Ohio River."

Corydon, Indiana, was just 14 miles across the Ohio River into northern territory, and as June progressed, so did plans for the town's Fourth of July celebration. Little did the good townspeople of Corydon suspect that the cannons used to commemorate Independence Day would soon be firing real cannon balls at Brigadier General John Hunt Morgan and his infamous band of raiders.

---

* Martha Ready was his second wife. He first married beautiful 18-year-old Rebecca Gratz Bruce in 1848, when he was 22. Always sickly and frail, Rebecca died 13 years later in 1861, the year the war began.

General Braxton Bragg, Morgan's superior officer, whom Morgan flagrantly disobeyed. Bragg was quarrelsome by nature and was universally disliked. In the space of one year, he managed to lose three battles: Perryville, Stone River, and Chickamauga — battles which many historians feel the south could have won under better leadership.

18

Chapter Two

Captured By Patriotic Horses

Morgan's idea, which was the possibility of crossing the Ohio River into the northern state of Indiana, was strictly forbidden by General Bragg, who had given Morgan permission only to strike anywhere he should choose in the neutral state of Kentucky, which included its largest city, Louisville. Although Louisville is in Kentucky, it is several miles *north* of Corydon, Indiana, because of the meanderings of the Ohio River. Louisville is about 25 miles northeast of Corydon.

Morgan confided his secret plan to his second in command, Col. Basil W. Duke, who just happened to be his brother-in-law. Duke was commander of the First Brigade of Morgan's Cavalry Division, and he quickly gave his approval to the plan. Duke had no compunction, either, against disobeying General Bragg. In his opinion there was a war to be won rather than a General to please. If, in fact, their plan were to be implemented, only Morgan and Duke would know their true destination; the men would not be told.

They had the foresight, however, to send two scouting parties across the Ohio River into Indiana to spy out the land. Morgan had heard reports that there were southern sympathizers, known as "Copperheads" and "Knights of the Golden Circle", in southern Indiana. Was this true? If so, how much

Morgan's brother-in-law, and second in command, Duke is remembered by historians as "one of the ablest soldiers who served the South." On June 19, 1861, he married Morgan's sister, Henrietta. Duke was a poet and an author. His book, "History of Morgan's Cavalry," written after the war in 1867, is the definitive reference on the raid. It has long been out of print.

help could they offer? Were the northern forces prepared to defend their Ohio River border? To what extent? Morgan needed to know, so he dispatched Capt. Samuel Taylor with one scouting party and Capt. Thomas H. Hines with another.

Taylor's trip was uneventful, but Hines and his scouts ran into a hornet's nest - the Corydon Home Guard - who captured the scouting party after they had, in effect, ridden into a blind canyon. Capturing the scouts was almost as easy as shooting fish in a rain barrel.

In spite of the *faux pas* about to take place, Hines was a capable and cunning spy. At the onset of the war, he had resigned his faculty position with the Masonic University at La Grange, Kentucky, and had formed a group known as the "Buckner Guides." He was soon commissioned as a Lieutenant in the Confederate Army, and he and his men served as advance scouts along the Ohio-Kentucky border.

Several months later, when his Guides were disbanded, Hines quit the Confederate Army in disgust. After about a month, however, he sought out John Morgan and offered his services. Although he reenlisted as a private, Morgan soon promoted Hines to captain and assigned him to lead Company E. From this company, Hines selected the men who would be with him on his secret mission into Indiana.

In Corydon, though unaware of Morgan's troops marshalled in Tennessee, much less of his plan to cross the Ohio River, the Sixth Regiment of the Indiana Legion, popularly known as the Home Guard, was issuing weapons and drilling. Led by Col. Lewis Jordan, Regiment Commander of the nine companies comprising the Harrison County Home Guard, the men grew restless as the tension grew.

One of the groups commanded by Col. Jordon, a veteran of the War of 1812 a half century earlier, drilled on the second floor of the old First State Capitol Building. The

Thomas Hines repeatedly carried the war north in a series of covert conspiracies. When one failed, or was betrayed, he would escape and plan another. He was perhaps the most clever, cunning, and conniving spy in the confederacy. It was Hines who masterminded Morgan's incredible escape from the Ohio State Penitentiary. After the war he became a newspaper editor, lawyer, and judge.

companies in the Home Guard, with their officers, were as follows:

Town of Corydon

Provost Marshal - Colonel John Timberlake
Henry Rifles - Major Thomas McGrain
Spencer Guards - Capt. George W. LaHue
Legion Cavalry - Major Jacob S. Pfrimmer
Legion Infantry Company - Major Leoida Stout
Legion Infantry Company - Capt. George L. Key
Legion Infantry Company - Capt. James D. Irwin

Town of Mauckport

Assistant Commanding Officer - Lt. Col. William J. Irvin
Mounted Hoosiers - Capt. William Farquar
Legion Infantry Company - Captain Huffman
Legion Infantry Company - Captain Hays

The Home Guard was to be put to the test a lot sooner than anyone thought. At 9 a.m. on Friday, June 18th, a courier, Sam Bruner, galloped in from Hardinsburg, Indiana, some 25 miles northwest of Corydon, with the report that about 75 Confederate guerrillas had left Hardinsburg and were approaching Corydon from the *north!* TURN OUT THE HOME GUARD!

How could Confederate guerrillas possibly be coming from the *north*? The Ohio River was to the *south*. But the report was true. They were coming indeed! Several days previously,they had sneaked across the Ohio River near isolated Alton, Indiana. For a cover, they had passed themselves off as Union soldiers looking for army deserters. Their ruse had worked until they were all the way to Paoli

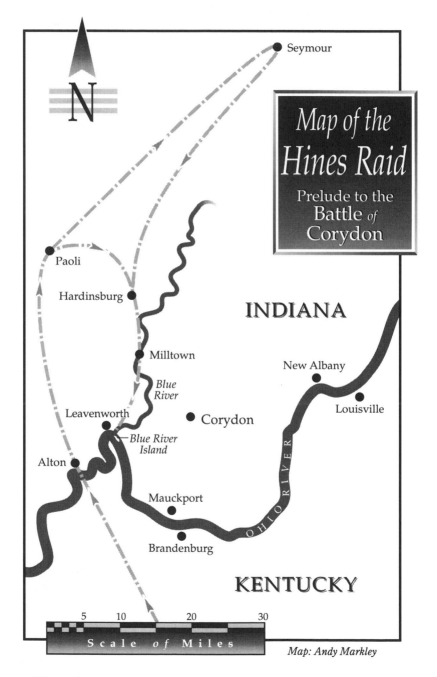

Seymour

N

Map of the Hines Raid
Prelude to the **Battle of Corydon**

Paoli

Hardinsburg

INDIANA

Milltown

New Albany

Blue River

Leavenworth

Louisville

Corydon

—Blue River Island

Alton

OHIO RIVER

Mauckport

Brandenburg

KENTUCKY

Scale of Miles

5   10   20   30

Map: Andy Markley

(one report put them as far north as Seymour), when their cover was blown, and they were recognized for what they were - Confederate spies.

Home Guard Commander Col. Jordon wasted no time ordering out two companies of Home Guards under the command of Capt. John T. Heth and Capt. George W. LaHue, as well as the Cavalry Company from Mauckport, 14 miles to the south. Lt. James Demoss assumed command of the Cavalry until Capt. LaHue arrived. Not only did the Home Guard turn out, they were joined by about fifteen private citizens armed with Henry 16 shooting rifles and other U.S. issued weapons. The Guard, augmented by the willing citizens, set out for Hardinsburg, only to be met by another courier who reported that the marauders had arrived at Milltown (which straddled the Blue River, the county line, which put part of the town in Crawford County and part of it in Harrison County) and were on their way to Leavenworth.

Cavalry, mounted infantry, and willing citizen volunteers, numbering about one hundred, started for the town of Leavenworth to the west. Capt. Farquar arrived from Mauckport with forty more men. The original courier, Sam Bruner, had gone on ahead and spotted the raiders' scouting party on Blue River Island in the Ohio River, a short distance from Leavenworth. From all appearances, they were stranded on the island, cut off from the Kentucky shore by the waters of the river, which had swollen considerably during the time they had been in Indiana.

Hines and his men had crossed over into Indiana near Alton, had traveled all the way to Paoli or Seymour, according to whichever account was accurate; then they had turned south to Hardinsburg. At this point, Sam Bruner, acting as the Paul Revere of the incident, rode to Corydon to spread the alarm. At various towns and villages along their route, the guerrillas had stolen fresh horses to replace their tired mounts. But their Hoosier horses, true to the Union cause, refused to swim the now swollen and rampaging waters of the Ohio River. As the Home Guard approached, Hines and his men were trapped on Blue River Island!

The story appeared in the June 23rd issue of *The Corydon Weekly Democrat* under the headline: THE GUERRILLA RAID INTO INDIANA - THEIR CAPTURE BY THE HOME GUARDS AND CITIZENS; It said, "Our citizens, though unused to actual war, showed the nerve of soldiers". The newspaper went on to report that the combined Home Guard units of Crawford County (where Leavenworth and Blue River Island are located) and the Home Guards from Corydon and Mauckport, assisted by citizens numbering several hundred, "invested" the island on the Indiana side, while the channel of the river held them secure on the other side.

The Home Guard opened up with their one gun, a six pounder, and when they got within musket range, the air was thick with lead. Ten of the Confederate raiders fell, mortally wounded. While the rest were hoisting a white flag of unconditional surrender, Hines himself struck out through the turbid waters of the Ohio River, endeavoring to swim to the Kentucky shore. Forty-nine men and forty-five horses were captured by the Home Guard, who returned to Corydon as heroes.

Yet, this was but a prelude to what Morgan, assisted by the wily Hines, with his now-gathered information, had in store for the Corydon Home Guard, whose nerve was soon to be tested again, only under much different circumstances.

Blue River Island

June 18, 1863
Morgan's Raiders: 10 Killed, 49 Captured
Home Guard: No Reported Casualties

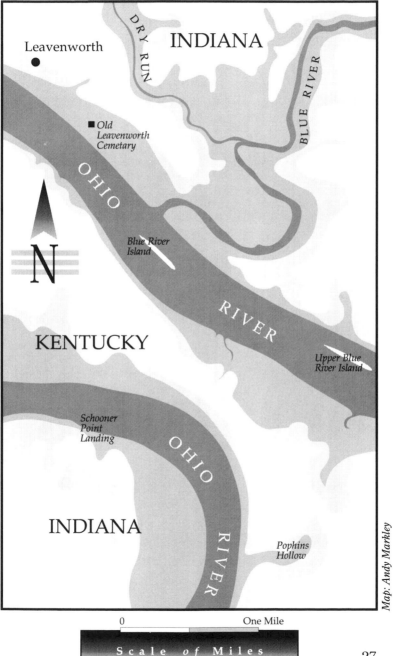

Leavenworth

DRY RUN

INDIANA

BLUE RIVER

■ Old
Leavenworth
Cemetery

OHIO

N

Blue River
Island

RIVER

KENTUCKY

Upper Blue
River Island

Schooner
Point
Landing

OHIO

INDIANA

RIVER

Pophins
Hollow

Map: Andy Markley

0   One Mile

Scale of Miles

27

Chapter Three

"Brother Cally,
They Have Killed Me"

During the month of June, the skies opened up over Tennessee, Kentucky, and southern Indiana. In northern Tennessee, where Morgan's troops were staged, the Cumberland River had risen out of its banks and was over half a mile wide.

But on June 10th the sun was shining as Morgan rode into camp, returning from a meeting with his nemesis, General Bragg. Morgan was dressed in a brand new uniform complete with all the gold braid of his general's rank. With his trademark, the elegant plume on his hat, he was described as "a most imposing figure in the saddle". As his officers crowded into headquarters, he told them simply that General Bragg had authorized another Kentucky raid, possibly as far as Louisville. They were to begin final preparations at once.

When he dismissed the meeting, he asked to see George Ellsworth. Actually no one ever called Ellsworth "George" - he was known simply as "Lightning" because of his incredible speed in tapping out telegraph messages. "Stick with me Lighting," Morgan ordered his clandestine telegrapher, "and be ready to tap into any wires we can find. I'll tell you what to say." Ellsworth, described as somewhat of a buffoon, couldn't wait to throw the Union forces into

George A. Ellsworth, Morgan's "Lightning". Described as a "buffoon", Ellsworth delighted in sending fictitious telegraph messages to confuse Union forces.

Telegraph key of the period - similar to "Lightning" Ellsworth's "bug".

chaos with his legendary fake telegraph messages, to which he often signed the name of either a Union officer or a railroad station agent. Lighting wasn't just fast — he was smooth.

Soon supply wagons were loaded with provisions, axles were greased, horses were shod by the blacksmiths, saddles were repaired, while the men grew tense waiting for the raid to begin. Yet, the rain still poured, and the Cumberland River they would have to cross kept rising.

As preparations were nearly completed, Captain Taylor, from the first scouting party, returned to camp with his report. He, too, had scouted into Indiana, and other than swollen rivers, there appeared to be no significant opposition. Unlike Hines, Taylor hadn't spotted any opposition on the Indiana side. He had, as instructed by Morgan, looked for the best places to ford the Ohio River, and he recommended one in particular. Brandenburg, Kentucky, should be ideal. There was nothing across the Ohio River in Indiana at this point except the small village of Mauckport.

Hines still had not been heard from, but no one, not even Morgan, suspected he had run into trouble. Morgan was determined to move out, swollen Cumberland River or not. He ordered the supply wagons and field artillery to be dismantled, loaded into flatboats, and ferried across the river. Four guns — two 3-inch Parrotts, and two 12-pounder howitzers made it. The horses and mules were driven into the river and forced to swim. All but a few made it. They were now in Kentucky.

A few scattered enemy patrols on the Kentucky side of the river offered some resistance, but only one of the raiders was wounded in the actual crossing. The resistance intensified, however, as they moved north of the river, and several of Morgan's men were killed. During this fighting, Morgan was again described as "sitting tall and erect in the saddle, with the flowing plume on his cap." If he didn't change his mind, he was on his way to the recommended Ohio River crossing at Brandenburg.

Back in Corydon, Indiana, while Morgan was crossing the Cumberland River in Tennessee, the Home Guard turned out again; this time it was a false alarm. Word came from Leavenworth at nine o'clock Sunday night: the raiders were back, this time with 900 troops! By eleven o'clock Col. Jordan had 200 men ready to go when they heard the signal — the tolling of the First State Capitol bell. Capt. Farquar and the cavalry unit at Mauckport were ready as well.

As the bell rang, the Home Guard started for Leavenworth and were all the way to Blue River Island before learning the report was false. *The Corydon Weekly Democrat* editorialized, "A beneficial result of the grand scare will show the rebels that crossing into Indiana is a very hazardous business - they may get into the state, but they cannot get out." The well-meaning editorial subsequently proved to be somewhat wide of the mark.

Just a few hours before Morgan had moved out his troops in Tennessee, he had received a table of organization drawn up by General Bragg:

Division Artillery Battery	CPT. E. Byrnes
First Brigade	COL. Basil Duke
2d Kentucky Cavalry	MAJ. T. C. Webber
5th Kentucky Cavalry	COL. H. Smith
6th Kentucky Cavalry	COL. J. W. Grigsby
9th Kentucky Cavalry	COL. W. C. P. Breckenridge
9th Tennessee Cavalry	COL. W. W. Ward

Second Brigade	COL. Adam Johnson
7th Kentucky Cavalry	LT. COL. J. M. Huffman
8th Kentucky Cavalry	COL. K. S. Clark
10th Kentucky Cavalry	COL. A. Johnson
11th Kentucky Cavalry	COL. D. W. Chenault
14th Kentucky Cavalry	COL. R. C. Morgan

The last name listed, Col. R.C. Morgan, was General John Hunt Morgan's brother, Richard. Three more of his brothers rode with him: Charlton, Calvin, and 18-year-old Tom. With his brother-in-law, Col. Basil Duke, that made five family members on the way to Indiana. But within three more days, there would be only four.

After crossing the Cumberland River into Kentucky near Burkesville and defeating the small resistance encountered, Morgan and his raiders camped for the night on the road to Columbia. The men sat around their campfires singing "My Old Kentucky Home". Within five more days they would, in fact, be in Bardstown, Kentucky, site of Stephen Foster's immortal Old Kentucky Home. Between songs the men cheered Morgan. They were pleased with his leadership, and he let it be known he was pleased with their courage and stamina. Morale was high.

Before dawn the next morning, July 3rd, they moved on north toward Columbia, where they were met by a Yankee Cavalry from Ohio, commanded by Col. Wolford. Wolford's men were no match for the Morgan raiders who soon sent them retreating. By noon, Columbia was securely held by Morgan. Next stop - ford the Green River and push on north to Lebanon. Near the river, however, they ran into northern infantry from, of all places, Kalamazoo, Michigan. The Michigan soldiers were no pushovers. Before Morgan

RICHARD MORGAN

Of John Hunt Morgan's four brothers who accompanied him on the raid, it was Richard who was made a colonel and given a cavalry unit to command. Richard with his 14th Kentucky Cavalry led the initial charge at the Battle of Corydon.

CHARLTON MORGAN

Another brother of John Hunt Morgan, Charlton was eventually captured and sent to the Ohio State Penitentiary along with his famous brother.

CALVIN MORGAN

Calvin was the Morgan brother who caught his younger brother, Tom, in his arms as Tom was shot through the heart. Eighteen-year-old Tom's last words were to Calvin, "Brother Cally, they have killed me."

THOMAS MORGAN

The youngest of the Morgan brothers on the raid, Tom's friendly demeanor and clear tenor signing voice endeared him to the men. His brother John's favorite, he was the first of the brothers to lose his life for the Confederate cause. He was just 18 years of age.

got across the Green River he had lost 36 men, with some 50 more wounded.

After pausing to bury his dead and line up a surgeon to care for his wounded, Morgan pushed on across the river, riding north through Campbellsville and on to Lebanon, where they spent the night of July 6th. The campfires burned bright and General Morgan's young brother, Lt. Tom Morgan, sang in his rich tenor voice for the pleasure of the men.

> *"When this here war is over,*
> *She's going to be my wife.*
> *I'll settle down in Alabam'*
> *And lead a quiet life."*

He sang another song, "We Sat by the River, You and I". The men loved Tom and often asked him to sing around the campfires.

The next morning a small Union force arrived in Lebanon; and seeing they were hopelessly outnumbered, they holed up in the red brick Louisville and Nashville Railroad Depot. Yankee sharpshooters positioned themselves at the depot windows trying to pick off some of the Confederate raiders before the inevitable surrender.

Soon a group of Morgan's men stormed the depot, including two of Morgan's brothers, Calvin and young Tom. Seconds before the Union soldiers inside the depot sent out a white flag of surrender, Lt. Tom Morgan passed one of the windows as he urged on his men. The last Union bullet fired from that window pierced his heart. His brother, Calvin, caught him as he fell. "Brother Cally, they have killed me" were his last words, and he slumped dead in his brother's arms.

Tom was gone. If Brigadier General John Hunt Morgan still entertained any doubts about invading Indiana, those doubts had just vanished.

INDIANA

OHIO RIVER

New Albany
Corydon
Louisville
Leavenworth
Mauckport
Brandenburg
Garnettsville
Bardstown
Elizabethtown

KENTUCKY

Lebanon
Campbellsville
Green River
Columbia

Map of
Morgan's Raid
From Sparta, Tenn.
July 1st, 1863
to
Corydon, Ind.
July, 9th, 1863

Burkesville

KY. / TENN.
STATE LINE

Cumberland River

Nashville

TENNESSEE

Sparta

10   20   40   60
Scale of Miles

Map: Andy Markley

Chapter Four

The Morgan
Shuttle Service

John Morgan had no way of knowing as he was burying Tom that things were not going at all well for the Confederacy. Within the last several days not only had Vicksburg, Mississippi fallen, but the biggest Civil War battle of them all was over. The south had suffered a crushing defeat at Gettysburg. The tide of the war between the states had taken a decided turn against the south.

Unaware of these misfortunes to his cause, Morgan led his raiders north toward Bardstown. They rode all night and arrived the next morning. After easily subduing the Bardstown Home Guard, they rested for two days in sight of the mansion that had inspired Stephen Foster to write of his Old Kentucky Home. As the troops rested, Lighting Ellsworth went into action.

He carried his "bug" and a coil of wire with him at all times. By cutting into a telegraph line, grounding one wire, and attaching his bug to the other, he could send and receive messages to his heart's content. Soon newspapers throughout Kentucky were carrying banner headlines:

MORGAN HAS 4,000 MEN; WILL STRIKE FRANKFORT

MORGAN HAS 7,500 MEN; TARGET CINCINNATI

LOUISVILLE OBJECTIVE OF MORGAN'S 11,000 MEN

After listening for a few minutes to the sending styles of other telegraphers on the line, Lighting could imitate them so well that his spurious messages went unchallenged. In telegraphy parlance it was known as a "good fist".

When Samuel F.B. Morse had invented the telegraph only two decades previously and had sent the first message over a wire, "What hath God wrought?" little did he dream that Lightning Ellsworth would be sending surreptitious messages over a similar wire to confuse the enemy in a war undreamed of as yet. Lightning used Morse's invention to its fullest potential. In succeeding messages he kept increasing the number of Morgan's troops and the number of guns; and he kept changing their destination. To say he had the Union forces utterly confused would be an understatement.

When Lightning completed all his fictitious reports over the wire, he listened for any results, and it was then he heard that pursuers were hot on their trail; indeed, only 24 hours behind. Morgan immediately moved his troops out of Bardstown and turned them westward toward Brandenburg. It was July 7th, and they still had 50 miles to go.

In December of the previous year, Indiana Governor Oliver P. Morton had ordered the 5th Volunteer Cavalry Regiment from Indianapolis to protect the Indiana Counties bordering the Ohio River from raids by Confederate forces. Companies D and L of the Regiment were sent to Harrison County and were garrisoned at Mauckport. After three months of routine patrol with no enemy action, they were ordered out, just four months before Morgan was to appear. Left to defend the Indiana shore at Mauckport, across the river from Brandenburg, was Lt. Col. William J. Irvin with his 100 man contingent of the Home Guard - "The Mauckport Rifles".

The raiders passed through Elizabethtown on their relentless ride toward the Ohio River crossing site at Brandenburg. There was no opposition. The Elizabethtown telegrapher had received a message, "No rebs here." Lightning had struck again. Ellsworth again sent enough bogus dispatches to convince any northerners that Morgan was on the way to *Louisville*. As he disconnected his bug, he cut the wire in two.

By 9 a.m. on July 8th, Morgan and Duke reached Brandenburg. The first order of business was to check out the swollen Ohio River they somehow would soon have to cross. First they saw the swift muddy water swirling around the boat docks. Next they saw an incredible sight. Nonchalantly leaning against a wharf boat at the landing, looking more dead than alive, was none other than Captain Thomas Hines. He was still worn out from swimming across the swift current, having made his escape from the Corydon Home Guard. Morgan was glad to see him. What did he have to report?

Hines, the master spy and manipulator of events, working non-stop the previous day, had helped set up the river crossing for the raiders. On July 7th, as the raiders moved out of Bardstown, Hines met other advance scouts, and they captured two steamboats. Seeing Morgan, Hines merely pointed, and as Morgan looked in the direction indicated, still another amazing sight met his eyes. Two steamboats were tied up at the foot of Brandenburg's main street with smoke rising from their stacks; and familiar faces appeared in the wheelhouses and on the decks. Morgan's *own men* were in absolute control of a shuttle service that would transport more than 2,000 men across the Ohio River! Hines not only looked exhausted - he somehow also looked smug.

He would soon relate the capture of the two steamboats, but first Morgan needed to know about conditions on

THE ALICE DEAN

One of the Ohio river steamboats captured by Brig. Gen. John Hunt Morgan at Brandenburg, Kentucky. After the crossing, Morgan ordered her burned so that the Union forces could not use her to pursue him across the Ohio River.

Copyright 1955 by Don D. John

the Indiana side of the river. Quite simply, Hines reported, there were no Confederate sympathizers to be found in southern Indiana; and they could expect no assistance from any Hoosiers. Furthermore, the Home Guard, though a determined lot, was certainly no match for the raiders. The crossing should go without a hitch.

An article in the June 30th edition of *The Corydon Weekly Democrat* echoed Hines report of no sympathy for Confederates. It read:

> "Lieut. Haycraft, second in command of Hines' company, captured at Blue River Island on Friday, stated to a number of persons that from constantly reading in a portion of the newspapers of this state that the Democrats were all rebels, he had been led to believe that he would have no trouble in recruiting a rebel company or regiment in Indiana, and that Capt. Hines did not doubt from these reports that he would be warmly welcomed by citizens of Indiana, and that they would flock to his standard. These same slandered and outraged citizens were among the foremost to meet Hines and drive him from the state."

The leaders of Morgan's two scouting parties collaborated on the steamboat capture. Captain Samuel Taylor[*], after his Brandenburg crossing recommendation had been approved by Morgan, took two companies, commanded by himself and Capt. Merriwether, and reached Brandenburg on July seventh. There they learned the mail boat, *John B. McCombs,* was due to arrive shortly after noon.

They lay in wait. Forty of the men hid not only around, but inside the wharf boat tied up at the dock, and the rest guarded the streets leading to the river bank. After lunch they heard the *McComb's* whistle signalling its approach

---

[*] Capt. Taylor was a nephew of Zachary Taylor, the 12th President of the United States.

from around the bend west of town. She was on time. Soon she would slow her engines, coast into the Brandenburg dock, and receive the surprise of her life.

As the gangplank was swung into place by the unsuspecting boat crew, forty shouting and yelling raiders stormed the boat; and, without firing even a single shot, they seized control of the *John B. McCombs.*

Her captain, crew, and some 50 passengers were dumbfounded as they were ordered off the boat. Yet, Capt. Taylor knew this one boat, prize though it was, would not suffice to transport over 2,000 men with equipment across the Ohio River. He needed another one as well. To get it he conceived a trap, with the *John B. McCombs* as the bait.

Chapter Five

Hobson Fiasco/
Morgan Coup

The next boat due to pass Brandenburg was the fast packet, *Alice Dean*, which would be coming from the east, down the Ohio River from Louisville. But Brandenburg was not a regular stop. Out went the bait, the *John B. McCombs*, into the middle of the river, where she hoisted a distress flag. The *Alice Dean* took the bait and hove to. River courtesy mandated helping another boat in distress.

Suddenly the *McCombs* spurted ahead under full steam on a collision course with the *Alice Dean*. It appeared the *McCombs* was trying to ram the boat coming to her aid. Veering at the last minute, the *McCombs* approached the *Alice Dean* on the port beam until the two boats were traveling side by side. It was only then the astonished crew and passengers of the *Alice Dean* realized the sailors on the *McCombs* were pointing rifles at them.

The two craft were lashed together with hawsers tossed off the *Alice Dean's* mooring bits. With the paddlewheels of both boats churning the water, they made for the Brandenburg wharf, where they tied up. Not a shot had been fired. The Confederate raiders, to their credit, treated the passengers with respect. Rather than acting as the thieves they were reputed to be, they opened the safe in the purser's

Brandenburg Crossing

July 8, 1863

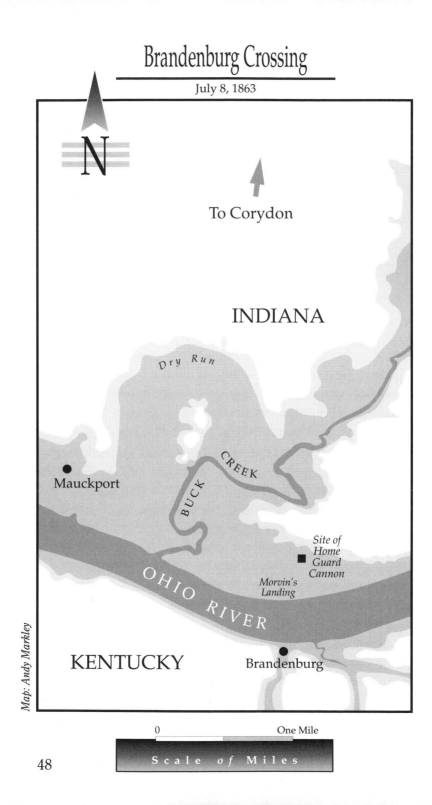

To Corydon

INDIANA

Dry Run

CREEK

BUCK

Mauckport

Site of
Home
Guard
Cannon

Morvin's
Landing

OHIO RIVER

KENTUCKY

Brandenburg

Map: Andy Markley

0   One Mile

Scale of Miles

office and returned, to the grateful passengers, the $10,000 they had placed there for safekeeping. The passengers of both boats were led ashore and were ordered to stay in Brandenburg; but they were given explicit instructions *not* to spread any alarm. The alarm, nevertheless, was sounded.

Another boat, the *Star Grey Eagle*, was tied up at the Tobacco Landing dock on the Indiana side, just five miles above Brandenburg. The Star's captain was shocked to receive this message:

> "The guerrillas or the advances of Morgan's army have captured the *Alice Dean* and the *McCombs* at Brandenburg. They are now lying there. You had better return to Louisville for troops."
>
> Signed
> William J. Irvin
> Lt. Col. 6th Reg. Ind. Legion

The *Star Grey Eagle,* immediately starting back up the river toward Louisville, met the steamers *Emma Floyd* and *Shenango* on the way. Both boats also turned around toward Louisville. All three boats were steaming *away* from the action, not towards it, which was a happy turn of events for Morgan. When they arrived at Louisville and New Albany, fire bells tolled the alarm, an alarm received too late to stop Morgan's river crossing.

The next boat due at Brandenburg was the *Lady Pike*, coming from Leavenworth. But Col. Irvin, who was at Mauckport on the Indiana side, was able to hail her before she reached Brandenburg and send her back to Leavenworth for help from that direction. Of course, Irvin had dispatched a courier to Corydon for Col. Jordan to bring in the Home Guard. Thus, help had been summoned from Louisville and New Albany on the east, Corydon to the north, and Leavenworth from the west. First to arrive was the *Lady Pike*, which returned from Leavenworth about midnight with an ancient six pounder and a detachment of thirty men from the Leavenworth Home Guard under the command of Capt. G. W. Lyons and Col. Woodbury.

The steamboat landed near Mauckport, and the cannon was manhandled to a bluff rising above the river, opposite Brandenburg. All through the night, the men struggled with the old cannon, floating it over Buck Creek on an old rotten boat, with the illumination for their frenzied work provided by nearby burning natural gas wells. As daylight broke through the fog, the old cannon was finally in place. But according to an eye-witness, who was, in fact, the First Lieutenant of the Mauckport Rifles, S.M. Stockslager, the men from Leavenworth never had drilled with the formidible old cannon so could neither handle nor aim it properly. According to Lt. Stockslager, had they known their weapon, the Brandenburg Crossing could have been forestalled. Here is Stockslager's assessment in his own words:

> "It will be recalled that long before the Morgan Raid a Regiment of Home Guards had been organized, armed and equipped under an Act of the Legislature, under command of Col. Lewis Jordan.
>
> The Company in that vicinity was called the Mauckport Rifles, of which Henry Hays, the father of Clay Hays, of Corydon, was Captain. I was 1st Lieutenant and James H. Current was 2nd Lieutenant. This Company assembled and marched to the front as ready for battle as any regular trained soldiers ever did.
>
> It is proper also to mention that an Artillery Company had been organized, under the law, at Leavenworth in Crawford County. It had received a small cannon, either that day or a day or two before, but had never had an opportunity to have any practice in using it. This Company with cannon, was sent up on a steamboat to Mauckport,

thence hauled to the point of crossing. Much rejoicing was occasioned by their arrival, as with the cannon we could begin the attack upon the unsuspected, probably sleeping enemy and so cripple his means of transportation as to, at least, hold them in check until Hobson could arrive and attack his rear.

If any man among the State's eager defenders slept, 'it was on his arms'. But probably none slept but watched for the breaking of day, which would usher in to many, their first real taste of war. I think I should mention that the river bottom lands just at the upper edge of Brandenburg presented, all through the night, a most brilliant and wonderful spectacle. Some oil wells had been drilled there, but no oil having been discovered, the great flow of gas from them was permitted to escape and in some manner was set on fire, making a constant blaze reaching apparently 30 to 50 feet high. The gas from these wells was subsequently confined and for some years used in evaporating salt water, which like the Corydon well, had fine salt water; later it was piped to Louisville. I am a little off my story, but these brilliant steadily burning lights, which burnt day and night, for years, made quite an impression on me, and perhaps others.

At last daylight came and soon the July sun rose clear and bright. All was eagerness on our side of the river. The little cannon was planted in front of an old abandoned log house standing a short distance back from the river bank. And no cannon shot ever rung out clearer- 'though not heard around the world,' than the first shot fired at the *Alice Dean*. It went high over the bluff or hill on the opposite side. Another charge and another shot, which also went wide of the mark. I think a third shot was fired with like result. By that time,the Confederates stationed on the hill opposite opened fire.

The first shot, as I recall, fell short; the second one struck the high bank just below the old house and the third one went crashing through it. This

Howitzer - a smooth bore cannon dating from the 1840's. Six pounders had a caliber of 3.67 inches and were five feet long. They fired a six pound cannon ball about 1,500 yards. Usually a "gun" fires on a flat trajectory, while a howitzer fires up into the air to lob the cannon ball onto the enemy.
Drawing by Ron Grunder

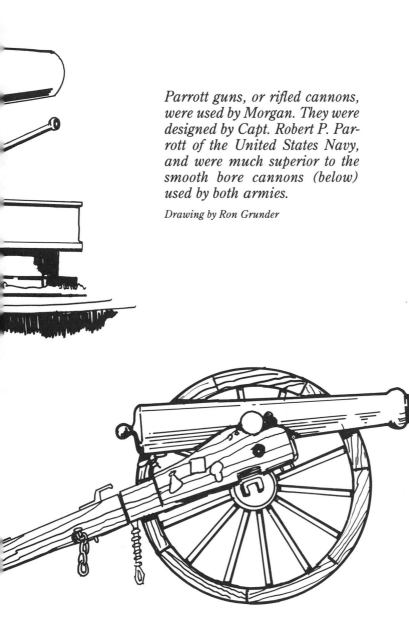

Parrott guns, or rifled cannons, were used by Morgan. They were designed by Capt. Robert P. Parrott of the United States Navy, and were much superior to the smooth bore cannons (below) used by both armies.

Drawing by Ron Grunder

Automatic Rifle

Drawing by Ron Grunder

TABLE OF FIRE. 6 POUNDER GUN

SHOT Charge 1¼ Pounds		SPHERICAL CASE Charge 1¼ Pounds		
ELEVATION In Degrees	RANGE In Yards	ELEVATION In Degrees	TIME OF FLIGHT In Seconds	RANGE In Yards
0°	318	1°0'	2"	600
1°	674	1°45'	2"75	700
2°	867	2°0'	3"	800
3°	1138	2°45'	3"25	900
4°	1256	3°0'	3"75	1000
5°	1523	3°15'	4"	1100
		4°0'	5"	1200

TABLE OF FIRE. LIGHT 12-POUNDER GUN. MODEL 1857.

SHOT. Charge 2½ Pounds.		SPHERICAL CASE SHOT. Charge 2½ Pounds.			SHELL Charge 2 Pounds.		
ELEVATION In Degrees	RANGE In Yards	ELEVATION In Degrees	TIME OF FLIGHT Seconds	RANGE In Yards	ELEVATION In Degrees	TIME OF FLIGHT In Seconds	RANGE In Yards
0°	323	0°50'	1"	300	0°	0"75	300
1°	620	1°	1"75	575	0°30'	1"25	425
2°	875	1°30'	2"5	635	1°	1"75	615
3°	1200	2°	3"	730	1°30'	2"25	700
4°	1325	3°	4"	960	2°	2"75	785
5°	1680	3°30'	4"75	1080	2°30'	3"5	925
		3°40'	5"	1135	3°	4"	1080
					3°45'	5"	1300

had the effect of scattering the whole force. There was a swale or low swamp-like space nearly a quarter of a mile back, in an open field, upon which there was a growth of small timber which served to furnish some protection, at least from view. Many persons took refuge in it, while others took such methods of getting away as seemed to them best. The Confederates opened fire upon the fleeing crowd and concentrated upon this little wooded space. It was then two of Harrison County's best citizens were killed by this amazingly accurate artillery fire, viz; Lieutenant James H. Current, a son of Garret Current, and Georia Nance, I think Nance was instantly killed. Current was removed, but I think died that night.

That inquiry is, if the Leavenworth Artillery Company had had one man who knew how to handle and aim their cannon, there can be no doubt they could have so disabled the *Alice Dean*, by a shot into her boilers as to have prevented her use for crossing, thereby delaying Morgan until Hobson could have come up and struck his rear, and possible [*sic*] captured his whole force, what might have been the effect?"

Lt. Stockslager's eye-witness account notwithstanding, the old cannon actually did some damage. It got in the first blow and drew the first blood. The very first shell tore through the upper rigging of the *McCombs*, which was making its first shuttle trip across the river. W.W. Wilson, quartermaster of Morgan's First Brigade, was wounded. This first cannon shot was quickly retalliated with fire from Morgan's Parrott guns. The Battle of Brandenburg Crossing, prelude to the Battle of Corydon, had begun.

The crossing, with multiple shuttle runs across 1,000 feet of water, by the *McCombs* and *Alice Dean* took nearly seventeen hours to complete. During this time, Union General Edward Hobson, with a force of some 4,000 men, was in hot pursuit of Morgan's 2,000 raiders, and they were narrowing the gap. Morgan watched from the old Buckner

Morgan's panoramic view from the Buckner home on the river bluff in Brandenburg, KY. Here Morgan watched the shuttle of his troops across the Ohio River onto the Indiana shore.

Mansion, high on a cliff overlooking Brandenburg, as the drama unfolded below. Even before the morning sun had burned through the fog rising from the river, the first shell from the old cannon on the Indiana side, after ripping through the rigging of the *McCombs*, landed on the river bank near the landing. For soldiers who hadn't had time to learn how to aim their cannon, they were doing pretty well.

Confederate Capt. Byrnes wheeled his Parrotts into position, guessed at the range because of the fog (as the boys in Indiana obviously also had to do), and sent off several rounds. One of the shots scored a bullseye and landed at the position of the old cannon on the Indiana shore. The two cannon servers, who had done their best, Lt. James H. Current of the Mauckport Rifles, and George Nance of nearby Laconia, lay mortally wounded. When the first group of Morgan raiders scaled the bluff, they found the cannon abandoned. The Home Guard had retreated, leaving the cannon in place between two haystacks.

But help was coming down the river from the east. The *Springfield*, a snubnosed tin clad boat shored up with heavy oak planking, was carrying three howitzers and had been dispatched from New Albany under the command of acting Ensign James Watson of the United States Navy. Watson fired his first shell at Brandenburg, then changed direction and fired his second shell at the raiders who had already made it across on the shuttle, landing on the Indiana side. Neither shot was effective, and there were no casualties. Morgan ordered his guns to open up on the *Springfield*. After an hour of exchanging fire, the *Springfield* ran out of ammunition and steamed back up river toward New Albany to replenish her supply. As soon as she was out of range, the shuttle continued.

But about 5 p.m. she returned, ready for another round. She had with her a sister craft, the *Elk*. But solid shots from Morgan's Parrotts kept them at bay. As night fell, they disappeared into the darkness. Then as midnight neared, the shuttle operation was completed.

Fearing, and rightly so, that his pursuers could use the *McCombs* and the *Alice Dean* to cross the river after him, Morgan ordered both boats to be burned. The flames consuming the *Alice Dean* lit up the night sky for miles, adding to the eerie glow of the 30 to 50 foot high flares from the burning gas wells. But fate intervened to spare the *McCombs*.

Col. Basil Duke, Morgan's second in command, happened to be an old friend of *McComb's* Captain Ballard, who agreed to take his boat upstream to Louisville so it could not be used to pursue the raiders. What was left of the $60,000 *Alice Dean*, after the flames had done their work, sunk to the bottom of the river, where it rests to this day.

Morgan's pursuers, 4,000 strong, led by Union General Edward Hobson, arrived at Brandenburg just as the *Alice Dean* slipped beneath the murky waters. Hobson's men fired a round at the departing rebels on the Indiana shore, who laughed, mounted their steeds, and rode north into Indiana. The shuttle was no more. Hobson was stuck with his 4,000 men on the Kentucky side of the Ohio River as Morgan and his men waved and pushed on toward Corydon. Hobson had missed his big opportunity by the space of just one hour.

If Hobson had not stopped, for whatever reason, at Garnettsville, just nine miles short of Brandenburg, while the Morgan shuttle was in progress, the shuttle could have been stopped in its tracks. Col. A.V. Kautz of the 2nd Ohio Cavalry termed Hobson's failure to push on for nine more miles the worst Union blunder in the entire chase after Morgan. As Hobson watched the laughing raiders fade into the Indiana gloom, with no chance for pursuit, it was not his finest hour.

The capture of the *McCombs* and the *Alice Dean*; the outgunning of the Home Guard cannon and the guns aboard the *Springfield;* the shuttle of over 2,000 troops with equipment across the Ohio; and, finally, the burning of the *Alice Dean* just as Hobson's 4,000-man force reached Brandenburg; or, in other words, the entire sequence of events during the last two days before the Battle of Corydon had done nothing to diminish Morgan's reputation as "The Thunderbolt of the Confederacy." He had just pulled off one of the slickest *coup de theatres* of the Civil war.

Union General Edward Hobson, who arrived in Brandenburg with 4,000 men just as the burning Alice Dean slipped beneath the waters of the Ohio River, was left stranded on the Kentucky side of the river while the laughing raiders rode north into Indiana toward Corydon.

Had Hobson not stopped at Garnettsville, just nine miles from Brandenburg, he could have prevented the river crossing. This command error was considered a serious Union blunder.

Chapter Six

On The Road Again

As the raiders left the swirling Ohio River and headed toward Corydon, 14 miles to the north, they were amazed to find the farm houses along the way abandoned, and apparently quite suddenly. Supper fires still burned on the hearths, and tables were set for the evening meal; yet, not a soul was to be found. Men, women, and children had taken to the woods.

Basil Duke stopped by a house at the side of the road where the door had been left standing wide open. "A bright fire was blazing upon the kitchen hearth," he was later to write in his book about the raid. "Bread half-made was up in the tray, and many indications convinced us that we had interrupted preparations for supper. The chickens were strolling before the door with a confidence that was touching but misplaced. General Morgan rode up soon after, and was induced to stop all night. We completed the preparations, so rudely abandoned, and made the best show for Indiana hospitality that was possible under the disturbing circumstances."

Duke neglected to add in his memoirs that before the *Alice Dean* was set ablaze some of the raiders had carefully removed the contents of the ship's wine locker, which included champagne. Their first night in Indiana was a merry one.

Some of the raiders hadn't been lucky enough to find a hastily abandoned house with food on the table, so they were hungry. Peter Lopp, who operated one of the grist mills along Buck Creek, was rudely awakened by a group of rebels demanding food. Lopp was a stubborn sort, which proved to be his undoing. He demanded payment for any food taken. The raiders offered to pay him with the only money they carried - Confederate paper money. Lopp refused to accept it. After carrying off a dozen barrels of flour, the raiders burned his mill to the ground. They then breakfasted on the flour mixed with water, plus salt and eggs they had "borrowed" from a nearby farm. The batter, fried in skillets over the embers of the mill, made a hearty breakfast.

With full stomachs, they mounted up; and led by Gen. Morgan's brother, Dick, they again headed north toward Corydon. Four miles south of town a shot rang out, and one of the raiders fell dead. The shot had come, they supposed, from the house of Reverend Peter Glenn, known throughout the area for his sermons opposing slavery. Without check-

Drawing by Violet Windell

Lopp's Mill on Buck Creek. Morgan's men burned the mill when Peter Lopp refused to accept Confederate currency for flour.

Confederate note given by Gen. Morgan to Pleasant D. Bean, who lived near the battle site. Morgan's men, while foraging for food in the Bean farmhouse, spilled a pitcher of cream on Mrs. Bean's new rug. Morgan insisted on paying for the rug with this Confederate banknote. Pleasant D. Bean is the great-grandfather of William "Bill" Bean, whose photograph of the Battle of Corydon re-enactment appears on the cover of this book.

Similar Confederate notes were offered by the raiders to nearby grist mill owner Peter Lopp, who refused to accept them for flour. The raiders then burned his mill to the ground.

Drawing by Violet Windell

Boone's Mill, built by Daniel Boone's brother, Squire, was the middle mill on Buck Creek. Morgan's men burned the first mill, Lopp's Mill, and many of the men camped overnight at the third mill, Frakes' Mill. Somehow the raiders overlooked Boone's Mill, and left it unscathed.

ing, the rebels fired into the Glenn home, killing Reverend Glenn and wounding his son. Then they set fire to the house and barn, both of which were quickly consumed.

The raiders pressed on toward Corydon. The Home Guard had been expecting reinforcements at any time from New Albany, some 20 miles to the east. Where were they? Perhaps Lightning Ellsworth's telegraph reports had so thoroughly convinced the New Albanians that Morgan was on the way to their city that they decided to stay home to protect their own citizenry from the rebels' treachery. In any event, the troops from New Albany never did come. If Morgan was to be stopped, it was up to the Corydon Home Guard.

At 11:30 a.m., the raiders ran into a barricade of fence rails about a mile south of Corydon. Behind the barricade,

A card game in progress in Boone's Mill. This picture was taken following the Civil War. As this book was published, Boone's Mill was still grinding grain, with the power to turn the two-ton wheel coming from the water flowing from the historic entrance to Squire Boone Caverns. The old mill is the focal point of Squire Boone Village.

This drawing by W. H. Shelton, which appears in a paperback volume entitled "Morgan's Great Indiana-Ohio Raid," depicts Morgan's right-hand man, General Basil W. Duke (mounted, foreground) volunteering to test pies left behind for his forces by housewives who fled at the Confederates' approach. The invaders suspected they might be poison.

armed with squirrel guns, muskets, and other ancient weapons, were about 400 men - the Corydon Home Guard, plus many willing private citizens determined to turn the raiders back.

As Dick Morgan's regiment charged the barricade, they were greeted by a volley from the resolute Home Guard. Within minutes, eight of the Confederate raiders lay dead, and 33 more were wounded. The only official battle of the Civil War, other than Gettysburg which was fought on northern soil, was in progress. The Battle of Corydon had begun!

Photo by Bill Bean

A re-enactment photograph depicts some of the raiders on the road from Mauckport to Corydon.

Re-enactment photo by Bill Bean.

Col. Richard Morgan led the first charge in the Battle of Corydon.

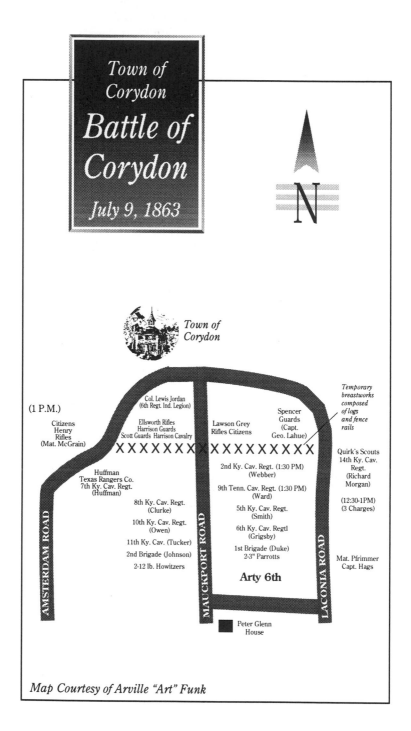

Town of
Corydon

**Battle of
Corydon**

July 9, 1863

N

Town of
Corydon

Temporary
breastworks
composed
of logs
and fence
rails

(1 P.M.)

Citizens
Henry
Rifles
(Mat. McGrain)

Col. Lewis Jordan
(6th Regt. Ind. Legion)

Ellsworth Rifles
Harrison Guards
Scott Guards Harrison Cavalry

Lawson Grey
Rifles Citizens

Spencer
Guards
(Capt.
Geo. Lahue)

X X X X X X X X X X X X X X X X X X X X X X

Quirk's Scouts
14th Ky. Cav.
Regt.
(Richard
Morgan)

(12:30-1PM)
(3 Charges)

Huffman
Texas Rangers Co.
7th Ky. Cav. Regt.
(Huffman)

8th Ky. Cav. Regt.
(Clurke)

10th Ky. Cav. Regt.
(Owen)

11th Ky. Cav. (Tucker)

2nd Brigade (Johnson)

2-12 lb. Howitzers

2nd Ky. Cav. Regt. (1:30 PM)
(Webber)

9th Tenn. Cav. Regt. (1:30 PM)
(Ward)

5th Ky. Cav. Regt.
(Smith)

6th Ky. Cav. Regtl
(Grigsby)

1st Brigade (Duke)
2-3" Parrotts

Arty 6th

Mat. Pfrimmer
Capt. Hags

AMSTERDAM ROAD

MAUCKPORT ROAD

LACONIA ROAD

Peter Glenn
House

Map Courtesy of Arville "Art" Funk

Chapter Seven

The Battle of Corydon -
Three Eye Witness Reports

The Battle of Corydon was not a battle of long duration. The Home Guard, without the help from New Albany they so desperately needed and were expecting right up until the last minute, were outnumbered four to one. They fought valiantly, like the brave heroes they were, and for as long as they could.

The author feels that the description of the actual battle can best be given by those who were there watching it take place. Three witnesses wrote their impressions of this historical event, and their accounts appear here just as they recorded them.

Our "war correspondents" include the Editor of *The Corydon Weekly Democrat*, himself a member of the Home Guard and an active participant in the battle; a respected Corydon citizen, and, finally, the battle as seen through the eyes of a 16-year-old school girl.

The First Report: CORYDON CAPTURED by Simeon K. Wolfe, Editor, *The Corydon Weekly Democrat*

About 11 1/2 o'clock on Thursday morning our scouts brought the report that the enemy was approaching in strong force up the Mauckport road toward Corydon. Our forces, consisting of about

450 Home Guards and citizens under command of Col. Lewis Jordan of the Legion, assisted by Provost Timberlake (late Col. of the 81st Indiana regiment) and Maj. Jacob Pfrimmer (who up to this time had been engaged with the cavalry in scouting) formed a line of battle on the hill one mile south of town, the extreme right wing resting at the Amsterdam road and the left near the Laconia road, making the Mauckport road, along which the main body of the enemy would approach, about one third of the distance of the entire length of the line from the right wing. The ground on the left of the Mauckport road is a heavy woods and though not hilly is somewhat uneven, which with the logs and underbrush made it difficult for a cavalry charge. This portion of the line was well selected for the purpose of saving our men from the rebel fire, but bad for the purpose of enabling our men to operate effectively against them, the line being at least fifty yards too far north, being that distance from an elevation in the ground which prevented either party from seeing the other before the enemy arrived to that distance from our line. Temporary breastworks composed of logs and fence rails were hastily thrown up by our forces which did good service in impeding the charge of the enemy.

About an hour later, the enemy made his appearance in small force, probably one company, about three quarters of a mile a little to the left and in front of our line where they were handsomely whipped by the infantry under the command of Captain G.W. Lahue which had been placed there for picket duty. In that fight we lost one man killed, named Steepleton, and had none wounded. The rebels had several killed and six or seven wounded. Before this skirmish was fairly over, the enemy made their appearance in front of our main line along the Mauckport road in strong force. We (the editor) were with a squad of the Henry Rifles under command of Maj. McGrain, at the extreme right of the line on the Amsterdam

Re-enactment photograph by Bill Bean.

The Battle of Corydon in progress.

road and had a full view of the approaching enemy. They completely filled the road for nearly one mile. As soon as they approached in range the Henry Rifles opened fire and did good work, the enemy being in full view. Soon the fire became general along the entire right wing, which checked the advancing column of the enemy, and compelled them to undertake to flank both our wings at the same time, a performance which the great disparity of forces enabled them easily to do.

Shortly after the flank movement was began [*sic*] and before it was executed, the enemy opened upon our forces with three pieces of artillery, making the shells sing the ugly kind of music over our heads. This shelling operation, together with the known fact that our line would be strongly flanked on both wings at the same time made it necessary for the safety of our men, for them to fall back. This was done, not with the best of order it is true, for our forces were mostly undrilled, but with excellent speed. From this time the fight was converted into a series of skirmishes in which each man seemed to fight upon his own hook mostly after the manner of bushwhackers.

In the meantime the enemy had completely flanked the town, having, before a gun was fired, taken possession of the plank road one mile east of town, where our men in their retreat were intercepted. Upon the right wing a large flanking force was sent against our lines and the fighting was very sharp for the space of 20 minutes in that quarter; twelve Henry Rifles and a squad of 30 or 40, some 100 yards to their left, armed with the ordinary rifle musket holding a heavy body of flankers in check for ten or fifteen minutes and compelling them to dismount.

Being completely overpowered by numbers, our forces gradually fell back to Corydon and the cavalry and mounted infantry generally made their escape. After the field was taken by the enemy they moved forward, and planted a battery on the hill south of the town, and threw two shells into the town, both of them striking near the center of Main Street, one exploded but did no damage. Seeing the contest was hopeless and that a continuance of the fight would only result in unnecessary loss of life and the destruction of the town, Col. Jordan wisely hoisted the white flag and surrendered.

The enemy immediately marched in and took military possession of the town; and then the work of pillage soon began. Everything the rebels wanted in the eating and wearing line and horses and buggies they took. The two stores of Douglass, Denbo & Co., and S. J. Wright and the two Steam Mills were the heaviest losers. The two stores were robbed of about $300 each and a contribution of $700 each in cash was levied upon the two mills in town and a like sum upon Mauck's mill near town. This large sum Messrs. Leffler & Applegate, Wright & Brown and John J. Mauck were compelled to pay to save their Mills from the flames. Many other citizens lost in horses and other property from 100 to $600, Mr. Hisey was robbed of $690 in cash. But we have not space enough to enumerate the pecuniary losses — few or none escaped entirely.

Losses.

The Union Losses, beside property, are as follows:

Killed:

Wm. Heth; Nathan McKinzie and Harry Steepleton — 3.

Wounded:

Jacob Ferree and Caleb Thomas — 2.

Our loss in prisoners was about 300 all of whom were paroled.

Re-enactment photograph by Bill Bean.

Gen. Morgan, at left, with his young aid-de-camp, surveys the battle scene as his raiders finish mopping up the Home Guard. Two of Morgan's men lay dead or wounded in the foreground.

The rebels admitted their loss to be 8 killed and 33 wounded.

Forces Engaged.

The number of forces engaged was 4,500* commanded by Gen. Morgan with 7 pieces of artillery. The Union forces, consisting of raw militia [*sic*] and citizens, did not exceed 450. With these raw troops — *one* yank to *ten* rebs** — Morgan's progress was impeded about five hours, which we hope will result in his capture.

Under all the circumstances we think our boys did exceedingly well. It was not expected at the start that so small a force could whip Morgan, but it was expected we could punish him some and impede his progress so that somebody else more nearly equal his strength could catch him and do him justice. That this will soon be done we have every reason to hope.

The Second Report: Personal Recollections of J. Edward Murr

When it became apparent that Morgan's Command was endeavoring to cross the Ohio river therefore it was understood that Corydon would be included in their itinerary and accordingly a hasty effort at organization and such other means and methods as might be devised were forthwith set going.

In the absence of telephones-runners on horseback were dispatched in various portions of the county. These were Paul Reveres on a very hot day in July. Farmers left their harvest-fields - merchants quit their places of business and all hastened to the threatened point of danger. It was decided to erect some sort of defensive breastworks just south of Corydon and since worm fences were then common these were generously

---

* The actual number was just over 2,000.
** The actual ratio was one to five.

appropriated. Perhaps no one about Corydon dreamed about a Rebel Foe as being any nearer than the dreaded Morgan Army but after the smoke of battle had all cleared away and folks had time to think things over they then recalled that Corydon was full of strangers. Pack peddlers, street corner men of all sorts and when the fort was being built and these strangers drafted to assist it was only subsequently recalled that while all natives carried at least two rails these peddlers only carried one each and when Morgan took the town the peddlers all turned up with him as pilots and scouts having been sent in to spy out the land and then disappeared at the precise moment prior to the attack.

Numerically the embattled Corydon farmers were strong enough to have put up such a stiff defense against Morgan had they been trained as to have turned him back altogether or at least deflected his march into other channels. But they were undrilled and undisciplined, and of course poorly armed. Comparatively few of the army of defense had ever been under fire, however a few had been Mexican war soldiers-some few Civil war veterans were at home at the time and among these now and then an officer. No one above a Colonel rank. It would be easy to criticize the defense from a military point of view but at least an effort was made. On the west of the town was a Company guarding the flank and these were under the command of Captain Harve Davis, a veteran of the Mexican war. Uncle Harve had been in battles with General Taylor when the Americans were one to five and yet came out victorious.

Mr. Davis deployed his command up and down a public highway skirting a deep woods. He was ready to fight or march to the sound of the cannon. After all had been placed and all carefully instructed to remain at their post the Captain started out on a scouting expedition to the south through this deep forest. After he had advanced some considerable distance he paused thinking he heard footfalls of a possible foe and judge his mortification on hearing these noises in his rear. He faced about fully expecting to meet a Rebel squad when lo, there was his entire command following their Captain fearing lest in his absence they might not measure up to expectation. On seeing them Captain Davis lifted his left hand high and said: "Boys go back, Go back! By jubits I'm reconnoitering the enemy!"

Many ludicrous incidents transpired and not a little pannicky spirit prevailed during and prior to the engagement. All sorts of wild rumors were rife, such as that Morgan carried a Black Flag and gave no quarter.

From first to last some two or three Rebels were killed and a few wounded on this Corydon Engagement. It is astonishing how many men claimed the honor of slaying a Johnie. Amos Burgess, a native of Virginia, ever maintained that he shot a Rebel just south of town and detailed the circumstances under which this transpired. Wm. J. Miles, who was a famous shot with his target gun, told me that during the onset of the engagement he was so situated that he perceived a sharpshooter behind a large poplar stump. The distance was great but be raised his sights took careful aim and killed the Rebel.

A Commissary Department for the Corydon Army was under the supervision of David Jordan, with headquarters at the Jordan residence. Bread, cakes, pies, meat etc., were gathered together in great quantities and Mr. Jordan was expected to issue these rations in true military fashion. In the midst of the performance of his complex duties he heard a shrill commanding voice ring out "I'll take charge here now and you get some tubs, buckets etc., and go to drawing water out of that well." On looking about Mr. Jordan perceived that he and his Department were surrounded by Johnies. He was thus made a prisoner at his own doorstep and through the whole of that hot July day he drew water for the men with Morgan.

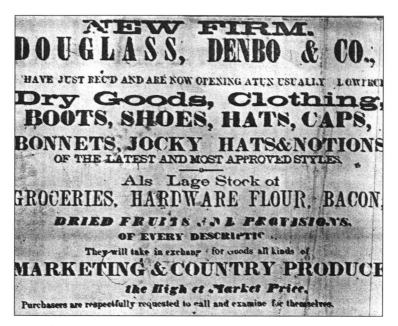

An advertisement in The Corydon Weekly Democrat, in the issue before the battle. After capturing Corydon, Morgan demanded of Douglass, Denbo & Co. the sum of $600.00 to spare the store from the torch. The store owners promptly paid the "protection money", and the store was spared.

Morgan's Command appeared in Corydon simultaneously from four directions. Joseph Pitman, a native of Virginia, and then a citizen of Spencer township, in a company with Mr. Colin, an old Napoleonic French soldier, reached the hill immediately north of the McGrain residence just as the Rebels were taking the town. Pitman was on horseback. He maintained his presence of mind and since he thoroughly understood the southern spirit he rode right through the command bowing right and left and greeting the officers in a fashion that they seemed to appreciate and he nor his horse were molested. The old Frenchman with military precision marched on too and he was not so much as arrested.

Morgan was very kind after all and human life and even property save horses all received rather careful attention. He might have shelled the town with his "Bull Pups" but he purposely threw the shells over the town, these landing upon Cedar Hill. These shrieking shells were quickly interpreted by the militia as an order to retreat and hundreds did so from the first. Guns, and in fact everything calculated to impede their hurried flight were cast aside. The Home Guards surrendered in a body, and were accorded some of the honors of war. Their guns were broken about trees, knives, purses etc. were taken. One man in company with a number of others a short distance from town, was overtaken and surrounded by a detachment. Just as the command of halt was heard this man remembered he had in his purse a large sum of money and he thrust his hand into his pocket, cast this purse at his feet, covered this with some sawdust which he perceived handy and after his release he returned to the spot and recovered his money. More or less brigandage characterized men of the command. Stores were entered and as might be expected the soldiers freely appropriated anything they pleased. But they went beyond the necessities of war and donned Ladies hats and bonnets, mounted their Kentucky steeds, tied ribbons to the horses tails and made considerable sport. One man was seen riding out of Corydon with seven pairs of ice skates on his shoulders, this notwithstanding it was the 9th of July and the weather sweltering. Morgan levied or assessed $1,000 each on the flouring mills. He indicated that by the payment of this sum protection would be given the mill and failure to meet his demand meant the application of the torch.

The owner of one of the mills on hearing this proclamation immediately called upon Morgan at the Kintner House Headquarters and handed the General a roll of greenbacks. Morgan carefully counted this money and finding $1,200 he handed the man $200 saying with a twinkle in his eye as he

Photo courtesy Indiana State Library

Morgan's Marauders stole a wide assortment of Hoosier property in their pilfering and plundering in southern Indiana, including birdcages, calico, hams, bread, chickens and ice skates!

did so: "Do you think I'd be guilty of cheating a man out of a cent." The owner of the other mill was not at Corydon and a neighbor paid the $1,000 but was never afterward reimbursed. Both properties were protected.

The Third Report: "Dear Cousin"

By Attia Porter, a 16-year-old Corydon schoolgirl, and daughter of Judge William Porter. A letter to her cousin, Private John C. Andrews, Forty-third Indiana Infantry Regiment, Company C.

Dear Cousin

I was just studying the other day whose time it was to write mine or yours and could not come to any satisfactory conclusion, when your letter arrived and as a matter of course I was the debtor and I have since found out I owe you two letters instead of one. I received yours with the miniature three weeks ago, but never could manage to sit down and write. We have had rather exciting times in Indiana for the last few weeks, and have had a few of the miseries of the south pictured to us though in a small degree. On the doubly memorable ninth of July a visit was paid to the citizens of Corydon and vicinity by Morgan and his herd of horse thieves. We heard Tuesday night that they had crossed the river and had disgraced the soil of Indiana with their most unhallowed feet. Our home guards skirmished with the rebs from the river to [Corydon] and on one of the hills overlooking the town had a grand *battle*. The battle raged violent for *thirty* minutes, just think of it! And on account of the large number of the rebs we were forced to retire which our men did in good earnest every one seemed determined to get out of town first but which succeeded remains undecided to this day. After the general skedaddle, Col Jordan wisely put up the white flag — and we were prisoners to a horde of thieves and murderers. I don't want you to think I am making fun of our brave home guards for I am not in the least. But now, that all the danger is over, it is real funny to think how our men did run. Gen. Carrington awarded great praise to us and we all think that is something. What could 350 undrilled home guards and citizens do against 4,000 well drilled and disciplined soldiers (?) We did not even know Hobson was following him. We sent to New Albany time and again for help and not one man or gun did they send us. Though we have found out since that it was the fault of Gen. Boyle and not the people of New Albany. It made Morgan so mad to think a few home guards dared to fight his men. I am glad they done it just to spite him. However they captured most of the guards and paroled them and killed three of our men. Father was out fighting with his Henry rifle but they did not get him or his gun. One of Morgans spies was in town three or four weeks visiting his relatives and some of his men helped our men to build the entrenchments. I guess none of the rebels down south are that accommodating are they? One of our brave boys run three miles from the rebels, and really run himself to death. He stopped at a house and fainted and never came to. Dident he deserve a promotion? I think that was the awfullest day I ever passed in my life. The rebels reported around that they shot father because he would not surrender, but it was all a story. The rebs were pretty hard on the copperheads but they did not take a thing from us. The[y] kidnapped our little negro and kept him three weeks but he got away from them and is now at home safe. We killed six or eight of theirs and wounded twenty five or thirty. I expect you are tired of hearing about Morgan so I will stop. I forgot my letter till so late this morning, and I have not got time to write much more or I will be too late for the stage so Goodby.

Attia

After Morgan's capture of Corydon, he made his headquarters at the town's finest hostelry, the Kintner Ho-

Kintner Hotel, Corydon, Indiana.

The Innkeeper's daughter entered the hotel dining room to hand Morgan a newspaper reporting the fall of Vicksburg and Gettysburg. Morgan was shocked by this news.

tel.* As he, with Duke and other staff officers were having lunch in the hotel's dining room the innkeeper's daughter handed him a newspaper with shocking headlines:

GLORIOUS NEWS!

Vicksburg Surrendered with Over 20,000 Prisoners!

The Great Battle at Gettysburg Penn. Between Gens. Meade and Lee—Lee Badly whipped.

The joy of the Corydon victory evaporated. The loss of Vicksburg and Gettysburg, Morgan knew, signaled a dim future for the Confederacy. Though crestfallen and depressed with this numbing news, he ordered his officers to round up the troops and move out. As he suspected, Union General Hobson had figured out a way to cross the Ohio River and was still in hot pursuit.

As the raiders prepared to leave Corydon behind, Morgan had one last item to attend to. He called for Lightning Ellsworth. "Send this message, Lightning: We're marching on Indianapolis. We'll burn the statehouse, sack the city, and release all the prisoners in Camp Morton.**

Lightning dutifully climbed a pole, cut into the wire, clamped on his bug, and tapped out another "Lightning Special." Indianapolis was thrown into hysteria. Of course Morgan soon turned east toward Ohio and rode *away* from Indianapolis.

---

* Today the restored hotel is a charming Bed and Breakfast Inn, and a National Historic Landmark.

** There were 6,000 Confederate prisoners in Camp Morton at Indianapolis.

Epilogue:

Morgan's Capture, Escape, and Death

The Morgan raid was developing into a raid of attrition. Morgan began in Tennessee with 2,460 men. By the time he left Corydon, he had less than 2,000. Those missing had been killed, wounded, or captured. On July 10th, the day after the Battle of Corydon, the raiders were 30 miles further north, at Salem, where they engaged the Home Guard, burned the railroad depot, and extracted ransom from the merchants to spare their establishments from fire. Then, instead of proceeding further north, Morgan turned his men eastward.

Before they crossed into Ohio, near Madison, they had been engaged in various skirmishes with Union soldiers and Home Guards, and their number was down to 1,500. With Hobson still only 24 hours behind them, they sometimes rode as much as 21 out of 24 hours. Morgan and his ever-diminishing number of raiders were becoming exhausted. One of his colonels muttered, "I'd give a thousand dollars for an hour of sleep."

By July 18th, the raiders were half way across the state of Ohio. Only 800 were left. For six more days the pursuit continued. As they neared the Pennsylvania border, they were down to 400 men. On July 26th, when they were near

Map: Andy Markley

East Liverpool, Ohio, Morgan, and what was left of his infamous band of raiders, could go no further. As he looked back, he saw a long cloud of dust getting ever closer. Hobson, after three weeks of relentless pursuit, had finally worn down and caught up to "The Thunderbolt Of The Confederacy." As Morgan announced to his men his intention to surrender, they dismounted from their horses and fell asleep on the ground. Even the wily Hines had *temporarily* run out of tricks. Yet, before our story ends, we will encounter Hines pulling two more daring, imaginative and bizarre escapes out of his trick bag.

Morgan and his officers were transported to Cincinnati the next day, where a throng of 5,000 people cheered as they were taken to City Jail. On July 30th, the prisoners were transferred to the Ohio State Penitentiary at Columbus. Incredibly, Hines was to mastermind a daring escape from this prison fortress. About four months later, on November 28th, the Secretary of War, Stanton, at his office in Washington, D.C., received the following telegram from Ohio Governor Todd:

> "I regret to announce the escape of John Morgan and five others from the penitentiary last night. They dug out under the walls. I cannot fault the military service with negligence. The warden and his guards alone are to blame."

Actually, Morgan and *six* others, which included Hines, had escaped! The morning after the escape, guards discovered holes in the floor of each of their seven cells. Hines left a note, partly in his favorite language, French, to taunt his captors:

> "Commencement Nov. 4, 1863, conclusion Nov. 24, 1863, number of hours of labor per day, five. Tools, two small knives; *La patience est Amére amais son fruit est doux.*
>
> T.H. Hines, Captain, C.S.A."

View of Ohio State Penitentiary, Columbus.

In the space of 20 days, they had, incredible as it seems, not only tunneled their way through the floors of their cells, but under the 30 foot high prison wall as well. Wily Hines had noticed the floor of his otherwise damp cell was always dry. This made him suspect there was an air chamber underneath it. Using knives smuggled from the prison dining room, he broke through the floor. He was right. He had broken into an air chamber running the entire length of the cell block! Then the others dug through their cell floors to the air chamber. At the end of the chamber, they started a tunnel under the prison wall.

For whatever reason, daily inspection of the cells had been discontinued. By November 21st, they had tunneled through 20 feet of earth and had tackled a four-foot-thick granite wall. They were through it in four more days. All seven escapees fashioned dummies out of bed clothing, which they placed in their beds. On November 27th, about midnight, the prisoners emerged into the cold rainy night. Within an hour they had boarded a passenger train at the Little Miami Railroad Station, a short walk from the prison.

They bought tickets to Cincinnati with money that had been smuggled to them in prison. Morgan took a seat next to a Union officer, who suspected nothing. But before reaching Cincinnati, Morgan and Hines, fearing their escape might have been discovered, jumped from the moving train into a Cincinnati suburb. The two men quickly crossed the Ohio River into Kentucky and disappeared. Two weeks later they emerged in Tennessee. Morgan was joined by his beloved Mattie for Christmas dinner. Only then did he learn their baby had been stillborn. After returning home, Hines married his long time fiancée, Nancy Sproule. But the adventures of the two cohorts were far from over.

Hines made his way to Richmond, Virginia, the capital of the Confederacy, where he was ordered by Confederate

Morgan and Mattie together after his dramatic escape from the Ohio State Penitentiary. Morgan was age 38, and his young wife 22 when this picture was taken. After Morgan's death, Mattie married a successful judge from Lebanon, Tennessee.

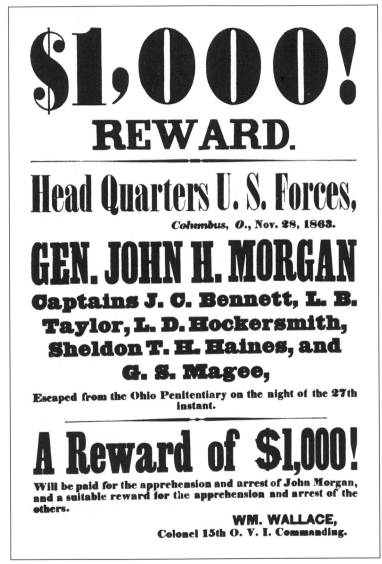

Reward Poster from the collection of Frederick P. Griffin.

President Jefferson Davis to Toronto to organize a subversive movement among the Canadians. When that plan failed, Hines endeavored to foment a revolution in Chicago and very nearly succeeded. However, a former Confederate officer, Lt. James Shanks, turned informant, infiltrated Hines' underground army, and disclosed the location of the Chicago hideout to Union forces. "A blacker-hearted villain never lived," Hines was later to write of the Confederate traitor Shanks.

With Shanks' disclosure, 3,000 Union troops descended on Chicago and captured all of Hines' men, except, of course, Hines himself. The cache of weapons confiscated in Hines' arsenal included 210 double-barreled shotguns, 350 Colt revolvers, 100 Henry rifles, 13,000 rounds of ammunition, and assorted knives and lances. They weren't playing games; they obviously meant business. Chicago was panicked. A dragnet for Hines, with a house-to-house search, was begun. Could Hines possibly escape again?

Of course he could! And this, his last escape, was probably the most bizarre of them all. Hines sought refuge in the Chicago home of Dr. Edward W. Edwards, a Confederate sympathizer and the leader of the Sons of Liberty. On November 7, 1864, at 10:30 p.m., Hines fell asleep in Edwards' home with a dagger under his pillow. At 1:30 a.m., Edwards awakened him advising that a Union patrol was in front of the house preparing to enter and search. It is difficult to believe what the conniving Hines did next.

It so happened that Dr. Edwards' wife was deathly ill with diphtheria, a highly contagious and often fatal disease. She tossed and turned with a burning fever. Over the protest of her husband, Hines actually climbed into bed with the gravely ill and contagious Mrs. Edwards. With his dagger he cut a large slit in the box-like mattress she was lying on, inserted himself down into the mattress *underneath* of the dying woman, and remained perfectly still. The Union soldiers searched the house, but they failed to look underneath of Mrs. Edwards.

The next day Hines slipped out of Chicago unnoticed. He never did develop diphtheria. Whether or not Mrs. Edwards survived is unknown.

After the war ended in 1865, Hines became the editor of the Memphis, Tennessee, *Daily Appeal.* He later was admitted to the Kentucky bar and not only practiced law, but went on to serve two terms as Chief Justice of Kentucky's Court of Appeals. In 1898 his wife, Nancy, died suddenly. Hines was crushed and could not be consoled. He followed her in death within three weeks. Considered by many to be "the most dangerous man in the Confederacy", Captain Thomas H. Hines died of a broken heart.

Meanwhile, John Hunt Morgan was up to his old tricks. Issuing the following notice, he organized a new group of raiders and staged another grandiose raid through Kentucky in 1864. Although the Confederate cause looked bleak, Morgan never stopped trying.

"Soldiers!

I am once more among you, after a long and painful imprisonment. I am anxious to be again in the field. I, therefore, call on soldiers of my command to assemble at the place of rendezvous. . . . Your country needs your service; the field of operation is wide, and the future glorious, if we only deserve it. Remember how many of your true comrades are still pining in a felon's cell. They call loudly on you for help. They expect it. Will you disappoint them? The work before us will be arduous, and will require brave hearts and willing hands. Let no man falter or delay."

John H. Morgan
Brigadier General, C.S.A.

Williams home where Morgan was killed. This picture was made shortly after the war.

The new raid finally led to Greeneville in Eastern Tennessee, and with the Federals on his trail, in hot pursuit as usual, he spent the night of September 3, 1864, in the Williams mansion in the center of town. He thought he was far enough ahead of the enemy to get a good night's sleep before he pushed on in the morning.

But as he slept, the enemy caught up, and learning his whereabouts, they surrounded the house. Had Hines been there, perhaps he could have pulled another trick out of his bag. But Morgan was on his own, and his luck had just run out. He tried to escape through the garden in the back of the house. As he tried to slip through the shrubbery, a girl watching from across the street called out, "That's him! - That's Morgan over there among the grape vines."

Morgan shouted, "Don't shoot! I surrender." Private Andrew J. Campbell of Company G, Thirteenth Tennessee Cavalry was closest to Morgan. "Surrender and be damned. I know you," Campbell shouted back as he pulled the trigger. As Morgan slumped to the ground, Campbell muttered, "I've killed the damned horse thief." Morgan died instantly, just as his young brother Tom had died a year earlier, with a bullet from a Union rifle through his heart.

This account of the Battle of Corydon and Morgan's raid has left unanswered a question that has stumped historians for one and a third centuries. Why? Why did John Hunt Morgan disobey orders, mastermind, produce, and direct a 34 day long pageant with a cast of 2,400 on a stage 1,000 miles long? Was it, as many historians believe, simply to divert Union troops away from other impending battles, thus giving the Confederates a greater chance of victories? Or was Morgan, as others believe, intoxicated with the grandeur of it all and gloried in the adoration lavished upon him by the South? Could it have been a colossal ego trip? We will never really know for certain. He was killed before he could write his memoirs. But whatever his reason for visiting Corydon on July 9, 1863, the Battle of Corydon will forever be listed in the archives of the War Department of the United States Government as the only official Civil War battle, other than the Battle of Gettysburg, that was fought on northern soil.

Pvt. Andrew J. Campbell, Morgan's assassin. After he killed Morgan, he was promoted to Sergeant.

Brigadier General John Hunt Morgan in 1864. His last known portrait.

Morgan family burial plot at Lexington, Kentucky.

Appendix A

Battle of Corydon Casualties
Compiled by Arville L. Funk

The known casualties of the actual fighting in Corydon and Harrison County were eight killed and six wounded. In addition, there were two known deaths that were a direct result of the Raid.

The Known deaths were:

LT. JAMES CURRANT (Current) — from Heth Township, wounded at Brandenburg Crossing July 8, 1863 and died the next day. He is buried at the Crossroads Cemetery near Mauckport.

GEORGIA (JEREMIAH) NANCE — from Laconia, killed at the Brandenburg Crossing. He is buried at the Beswick Cemetery, (Radmaker Farm, east of Laconia).

NATHAN MCKINZIE — killed at the Battle of Corydon, July 9, 1863, buried at Buttontown Cemetery, 2 miles south of Greenville, Floyd County, Indiana.

HARRISON STEEPLETON — killed at the Battle of Corydon, buried at Union Chapel, Boone township.

COL. JACOB FERREE — wounded at Battle of Corydon, died several days later buried on his farm in Boone Township.

ISAAC LANG — died from a heart attack suffered in the retreat from the Battle of Corydon, July 9, 1863.

WILLIAM HETH — Toll Road keeper, killed at his toll gate on the east edge of Corydon on the New Albany Toll Road (Rd. 62). Killed July 9, 1863 and buried at Cedar Hill Cemetery, Corydon.

REV. PETER GLENN — Lutheran minister, killed at his farm, four miles south of Corydon, buried at Jordan's Cemetery, just across the road from his farm.

MISS ABBIE SLEMONS — died in August, 1863 as a result of the hardship and exhaustion during the raid.

MRS. CYNTHIA BOOKER DENBO — died of exhaustion on July 16, 1863 as a result of the raid.

Re-enactment photograph by Bill Bean.

Col. John Hunt Morgan, right, along with a veteran of the battle, looks over a monument erected at the battle site to commemorate the Confederate soldiers who lost their lives in the battle.

CAPT. WILLIAM FARQUAR — injured in an accident in the fight at the Brandenburg Crossing, July 8, 1863.

JOHN GLENN — son of Rev. Glenn, wounded in both legs in the fight at his father's house, four miles south of Corydon.

CALEB THOMAS — wounded in the Battle of Corydon.

Also three other Home Guards wounded at the Brandenburg Crossing.

In addition to the known casualties, there were reported several deaths that cannot be confirmed because of lack of accurate details.

The true Confederate losses will probably never be known. Official records state: at least eight were killed and approximately forty were wounded.

The known Confederate losses were:

PVT. ALBERT WOMACK — 9th TN Cav., died of wounds suffered in the Battle of Corydon. Body buried at Cedar Hill Cemetery, Corydon, later returned, to McMinnville, TN., his home.

PVT. GREENE BOTTOMER — killed at the Battle of Corydon, buried at Cedar Hill Cemetery, Corydon.

CAPT. W. H. WILSON — Quartermaster, 1st Brigade, wounded in Brandenburg Crossing.

LT. P. H. THORPE — Co. A, 2nd KY Cav., wounded at Battle of Corydon.

PVT. ARTHUR JOHNSON — 2nd KY Cav., wounded at Battle of Corydon.

PVT. CHARLES BEST — 2nd KY Cav., wounded at Battle of Corydon.

PVT. LEN A SHARP - Co. A. 8th KY Cav., wounded at Battle of Corydon.

Photograph from the collection of Fred P. Griffin.

PVT. R. S. PORTER, Co. C., 2nd KY Cav., wounded at Battle of Corydon.

The other Confederate dead were probably buried at the old Edward Smith farm on the south hill, and now no traces remain of the old graveyard.

The old Presbyterian Church building, which stood on south Capitol Avenue was used as a hospital for Morgan's Confederate wounded and dying soldiers. That night, after the last of the Confederate Raiders had galloped on north toward Salem, those wounded of Morgan's number who were left behind in Corydon were cared for by the towns-people until they were able to return south. As was told years ago by many of the older citizens of Corydon: "Those of Morgan's men who were left behind were nursed and cared for by the citizens of Corydon and not one of Morgan's wounded were molested or mistreated by the local citizens."

Appendix B
Corydon Today

Photograph by Bill Bean

ALL ABOOOOAAAARRD!

The Corydon Scenic Railroad, built not long after the Civil War, leaves Corydon for a one and one-half hour adventure through the scenic countryside, following the route of Gen. Morgan and his Raiders as they left Corydon on July 10, 1863, and headed north toward Salem. The Depot is in downtown Corydon.

With an official 1990 population of 2,628, the town of Corydon, nestled in southern Indiana's Lincoln Hills, remains just as charming as ever, and each year hosts over a quarter million visitors*. The historic downtown area acts as a magnet to draw visitors from all 50 states and many foreign countries. Not only the battle site, but the *entire town* has been designated by the Department of the Interior as a National Historical Landmark.

In addition to tours of the historic First State Capitol and Governor Hendricks' House conducted by the State of Indiana Museum System, visitors enjoy the many quaint gift shops, craft shops, and antique shops around the Town Square and throughout the downtown area. At the Zimmerman Art Glass Factory, visitors watch craftsmen producing paperweights, vases, and other glass art objects, using the same method as our Colonial ancestors.

Down at the depot, the Conductor shouts, "All Aboard" as the passenger train pulls away from the station for a 16 mile trip through the scenic countryside. Walking tours of the historic downtown area are popular. Complete information on all the historic sites is available at the Tourist Information Center on the Square, open daily. Nostalgic horse-drawn carriage rides through the historic district are also available, as are bus tours.

The site of the Battle of Corydon, one mile south of town, where the Home Guard did their best to hold back the infamous Morgan's Raiders on July 9, 1863, is a popular destination. The battlefield includes plaques and markers.

---

* Includes visitors to the three nearby caves.

Corydon Walking Tour

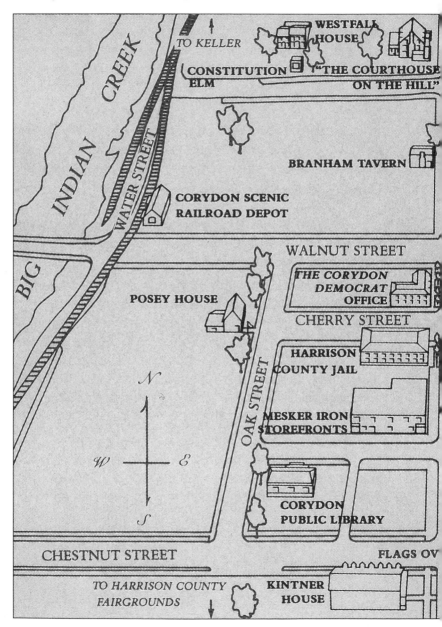

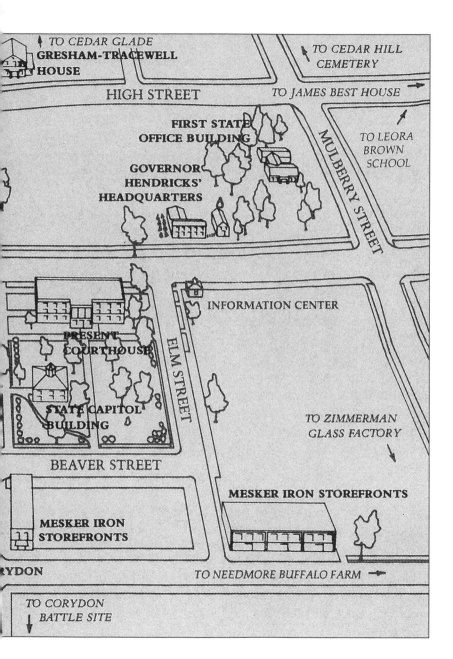

The Courthouse on the Hill

In 1811, an unfinished log house on this site was purchased by Harrison County to serve as its first Courthouse. When the territorial capital moved from Vincennes to Corydon in 1813, territorial officers shared the quarters with the Harrison County officials. Forty-three delegates from the Indiana Territory's 13 counties met in "The Courthouse on the Hill" in June 1816 to draw up Indiana's first constitution. With cramped indoor quarters, the delegates chose the inviting shade of the nearby giant elm tree. Near the elm was a spring with cool water for drinking and an excellent spot to cool their jugs of brandy. The present house was built in 1917 and is a private residence.

*The Constitution Elm

In the hot June of 1816, Indiana delegates met under the spreading branches of one of the largest elms of its kind in the world to draft Indiana's first state constitution. This magnificent tree, with a trunk 5 feet across and branches 132 feet from tip to tip, stood 50 feet tall. In 1925, it became a victim of the elm beetle. The limbs were removed, and the trunk was enclosed by a sandstone memorial erected by the State to mark it as a significant Hoosier monument.

The Westfall House

This house, directly behind the Elm, is one of the oldest houses in Corydon. Constructed of logs in 1807 by the Westfall family, it was later occupied by Col. Lewis Jordan, who commanded the Corydon Home Guard during the Battle of Corydon in 1863. Today it is a private residence.

*open for visitors

The Corydon Democrat Office

Established in 1856, the weekly newspaper *The Corydon Democrat* purchased its present office from Cora Slemons Morris in 1911. This building, a fine example of federal style architecture, was built in 1842 by Mrs. Morris' father, Dr. John Slemons, to serve as his residence and drug store.

Harrison County Jail

Harrison County's first jail was constructed of logs at this site in 1809. Until 1823, the whipping post in front of the jail was used for public punishment. On June 12, 1889, a band of vigilantes known as "White Caps" removed two men accused of burglary and lynched them on the West Bridge. The present building was erected in 1969.

*The Posey House

In 1817, the Posey family built a massive brick house in the shape of a "U". Col. Thomas Posey, son of Indiana's last territorial governor, lived here until shortly before his death in 1863. Although he did not marry, he reared 14 orphaned children here. The Daughters of the American Revolution now operate it as a museum.

First State Office Building

Built in 1817, this brick building was rented to the State of Indiana for offices while Corydon was capital (1816-1825). The east room was occupied by the State Auditor and the west room by the State Treasurer. The cellar under the west room was used as the Treasury Vault, where the money, in silver, was kept in strongboxes. Formal State

*open for visitors

Balls were held here, the furniture being moved into the yard on such occasions. Today it is a private residence.

*The Kintner House

The original Kintner House stood at the northwest corner of Capitol Avenue and Beaver Street. The hotel was used as headquarters by Gen. John Morgan, a Rebel Raider, after he captured Corydon on July 9, 1863. This building burned shortly after the Civil War, and a new hotel was erected one block south. It was operated by the Kintner family and was the town's leading hotel for many years. Restored in 1986, it is now a bed and breakfast.

Leora Brown School

Built in the 1890's for the education of black children, the grade school was housed in one room and the high school in the other. High school students were integrated into the white school in the 1930's and grade school children in the 1950's. This may be the oldest former black school building still standing in Indiana.

*Branham Tavern

This two-story log structure was built by Gov. William Henry Harrison in 1800. William Branham was licensed to keep a tavern here on April 4, 1809. In October 1821, the Indiana Gazette announced that one Eleazor Goodwin opened "a House of Public and private entertainment . . . at the old stand formerly occupied by William Branham . . . "

open for visitors

*Governor Hendricks' Headquarters

This two-story federal style brick house was built in 1817. William Hendricks made the house his headquarters and home while he was governor of Indiana (1822-1825). In 1841 Judge William A. Porter acquired the house, which remained in his family until the state secured it and opened it to the public in 1979.

*The State Capitol Building

This foremost of Corydon's landmarks is constructed of rough blue limestone which was quarried locally. The walls are 2 1/2 feet thick on the first floor and 2 feet thick on the second floor. The building is 40 feet square. It was completed in 1816 at a cost of $3,000, of which $301 was paid with the salvage value of "The Courthouse on the Hill." The House of Representatives occupied the lower room, the Senate Chamber and the Supreme Court the upstairs. When the legislature was not in session, the County and District courts utilized the building. The capital was moved to Indianapolis in 1825.

Mesker Iron Works

Downtown Corydon has on many of its store fronts a display of architectural iron from the George L. Mesker and Company Iron Works of Evansville, Indiana. This type of ornamental iron was in vogue during the 1890s. Examples of its use can be seen on the north side of Chestnut Street and the Square.

open for visitors

*The Corydon Public Library

In Corydon's State Capital days, residents were obliged to borrow their reading matter from the lending library in Jack and Sarah Jamison's tavern on Chestnut Street. A Harrison County Library existed from 1839 to 1878. The present library, financed by the Carnegie Fund, was built in 1914. During the interim, various lending libraries were made available, including a McClure Working Men's Institute Library. The library has an extensive genealogy section.

*The Present Courthouse

On February 25, 1928, Harrison County laid the cornerstone for a new three-story courthouse which was dedicated May 4, 1929. Harrison County is unique in that original records and documents, mostly handwritten, dating back to Corydon's inception in 1808, have been preserved and protected in this building.

*Flags Over Corydon

The 35 Flags on display all flew over the Corydon area at one time. Each flag has been researched and documented by the Smithsonian Institution.

The Gresham-Tracewell House

Lawyer Walter Q. Gresham (Civil War General, Fed. Judge and Secretary of State) lived here in the 1860s. The house was also the boyhood home of Robert Tracewell, Comptroller of the U.S. Treasury under Presidents McKinley, Roosevelt, Taft and Wilson.

open for visitors

Other Interesting Sites Close to Downtown Corydon

*Cedar Hill Cemetery

Cedar Hill Cemetery contains the graves of soldiers from the American Revolution and all succeeding wars, including graves of confederate soldiers from the Battle of Corydon. Many black slaves are buried here; some have marked graves, but many others are buried in graves marked only by a rough creek stone slab. The earliest established burial date is 1807, the year before Corydon was officially founded.

Cedar Glade

This stately house, built in 1808, was used as a refuge during Morgan's Raid in 1863 because it was the farthest point from the battle. Ironically, cannonballs fired over the town fell in the yard. The McGrain family has maintained the property as their private residence since 1849.

*Live Entertainment

Weekend performances are given by local or regional talent at the Indian Creek Theatre. Country, bluegrass, gospel, orchestra, jazz and more! Seats 750. For information call 812-738-1234. The Corydon Jamboree, "Corydon's #1 Music Show" features a Country performance every Saturday night. For information call 812-969-2049 or 502-422-3122

*open for visitors

*The Harrison County Fairgrounds

The Harrison County Fair is the oldest continuous fair in Indiana, dating from 1860. At the southwest corner of the fairgrounds is a spring marking the location of the first permanent home in Corydon. A natural amphitheater is nearby. Harness race horses can be seen exercising on the half-mile track. The property is privately owned by the Harrison County Agricultural Society, Inc.

Keller Manufacturing Company

Farm wagons made in Corydon by Keller Manufacturing Company were shipped to every state of the Union and seven foreign countries. The first wagons from the Keller factory were sold in 1901. Since 1942, the company has developed an extensive line of household furniture. Keller furniture is sold throughout the U.S.

The James Best House

Built in 1904, this house became the childhood home of actor James Best, who is well known as Roscoe P. Coltrain, sheriff on the television series *Dukes of Hazard*.

*The Village Blacksmith

This ornamental ironworks handcrafts everything form wrought iron napkin holders to park benches plus custom orders. Open 10:30-5:00 Saturday and 11:30-5:00 Sunday, May-October. Located on High Street across from the Constitution Elm.

*open for visitors

*Site of the Battle of Corydon

Here the Corydon Home Guard met the main force of Gen. John Hunt Morgan's Confederate Raiders on July 9, 1863. Morgan drove the greatly outnumbered Home Guard back, planted cannons on the south hill and shelled the town. The Rebel forces suffered eight killed and 33 wounded, and Home Guard had four casualties and eight wounded. This battle was one of two Civil War battles fought on Northern soil. While in Corydon, Gen. Morgan received word of the South's defeat at the Battle of Gettysburg, Pennsylvania.

Information concerning local collections of Indian artifacts, heirloom quilts, rare circus music and other points of interest is available at the Visitors' Center on the corner of Walnut and Elm Streets.

---

*open for visitors

Millions of years in forming, the "Rock of Ages" column dominates the "Rotunda Cathedral" room in Squire Boone Caverns, which was discovered by brothers Daniel and Squire Boone in 1790. Squire Boone is buried in the cave.

Indiana Cave Country

Corydon is the hub of "Indiana Cave Country" and is surrounded by three of the most outstanding show caves in America, each with a personality of its own. South of Corydon is Squire Boone Caverns, noted for its roaring underground rivers and waterfalls, which highlight thousands of dazzling formations. A craft village with working grist mill is part of the attraction.

Northwest of Corydon is Marengo Cave, with two different tours, one of which includes "The Crystal Palace", one of the most beautiful rooms in any American cave. Marengo also offers horseback riding and canoe trips on the Blue River.

A scene in the Crystal Palace section of Marengo Cave.

119

The world's tallest underground mountain in Wyandotte Cave.

West of Corydon are Wyandotte Caves, operated by the State of Indiana, which contain the largest known underground mountain, as well as an outstanding display of helectites, the curious formations which defy gravity. All three caves are approved by the National Caves Association and offer guided tours which leave at frequent intervals. The caves are electrically lighted and include safe walkways with handrails. The temperature in the caves is a pleasant 58 degrees year round.

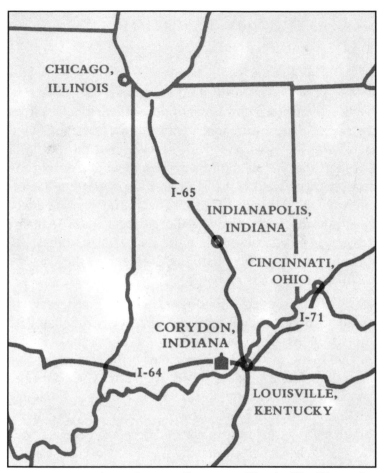

Located approximately 20 miles west of Louisville, Kentucky, Corydon is easily accessible from several Interstate Highways. Scenic Indiana Interstate 64 runs just north of Corydon. Exit onto State Road 135 South, then onto State Road 337 South, which leads directly into the historic district.

Acknowledgements

During the two years of research to find material for this book, it has been exciting to uncover fact after fact, many of them little known, and to weave them together from the perspective of Corydon, as fine a town as can be found anywhere. I was surprised to discover that the Battle of Corydon was but one of *three* battles in which, during the span of three weeks, the Harrison County Home Guard engaged the Morgan Raiders. The Battle of Blue River Island and the Battle of Brandenburg Crossing were equally, if not even more, colorful than the Battle of Corydon itself, the only one of the three battles to be listed by the War Department as an "official" battle.

The encouragement and assistance I received researching and writing this book have certainly been gratifying. The late Arville "Art" Funk, acknowledged as the foremost expert on the Battle of Corydon, graciously made available his various books and articles. I deeply regret that he did not get to review the manuscript for this book before his untimely death. Frederick P. Griffin, Harrison County's Official Historian, reviewed the manuscript and made excellent suggestions. Bill Brockman, Assistant Curator, Corydon Capitol State Historic Site, verified various historical facts and assisted in the research.

Dan Bays, Corydon Public Librarian, could not have been more helpful. He not only made the archives of the library available to me; he assisted in recreating copies of *The Corydon Weekly Democrat* newspapers from microfilm of various issues in June and July, 1863. William M. "Bill" Bean, photographer extraordinaire, let me choose from dozens of his excellent photographs of the battle re-enactment.

ACKNOWLEDGEMENTS

Former artist-in-residence at Squire Boone Village, Violet B. Windell was kind enough to permit the use of several of her excellent pen and ink drawings.

Of the many persons who encouraged me in this undertaking, one stands out above the others. Blaine Wiseman, retired President of Corydon's Old Capitol Bank, not only encouraged me with this project, but with many other endeavors over the years. A finer gentleman I have never met.

Several drafts of the manuscript were put on word processor by Pam Jones, who then did the typesetting and layout. Her avid interest was heartening. Andy Markley did a great job with the maps from sketches I supplied. Ron Grunder, using a Bill Bean photograph, created the book cover. My wife, Betty, who has edited many books for others, got the opportunity to edit a book for her husband, and, as usual, did a superb job.

W. Frederick Conway, Sr.

Index

126

About the Author

Fred Conway is holding a rare book about Morgan's Raid, originally owned by the grandson of Col. Basil Duke, Morgan's second in command, as well as his brother-in-law.

W. Fred Conway, Sr., a writer and historian by avocation and an industrialist by vocation, has business interests in both Harrison County, Indiana, and neighboring Floyd County, which until 1819 was part of Harrison County.

He was the original developer of Squire Boone Caverns near Corydon, now owned by his son, Rick, who has expanded it into a Craft Village whose "1804 Brand" of products are sold at more than 10,000 gift shops across America.

For many years Fred Conway has been the first trombonist with the Corydon Concert Band, which plays Friday evening concerts on the town square during the summer season. His son, Rick, plays the euphonium in the band, and Rick's son, Derick, is ready to join as a trombonist. Fred Conway's grandfather was a trombonist and the director of the Listonburg town band in Pennsylvania during the 1880's. Thus, a span of five generations covers more than a century of fulfilling the town band tradition in America.

Mr. Conway, a life-long fire buff, and a former Fire Chief, maintains a museum of antique fire engines and equipment at the Conway Enterprises industrial plant in nearby New Albany, Indiana where his other two children, Allen and Winifred hold the respective positions of Chief Operations Officer and Vice President of Administration. Other of his books include histories of various types of fire engines and firefighting equipment used in times past.

He is a graduate of Duke University, with majors in Music and English. He and his wife Betty live near Floyds Knobs, Indiana.